MANUAL

Stephen Kieran
James Timberlake

Princeton Architectural Press
New York

May 2002

gantmelle.

Stephen Kieran

FOR OUR PARENTS

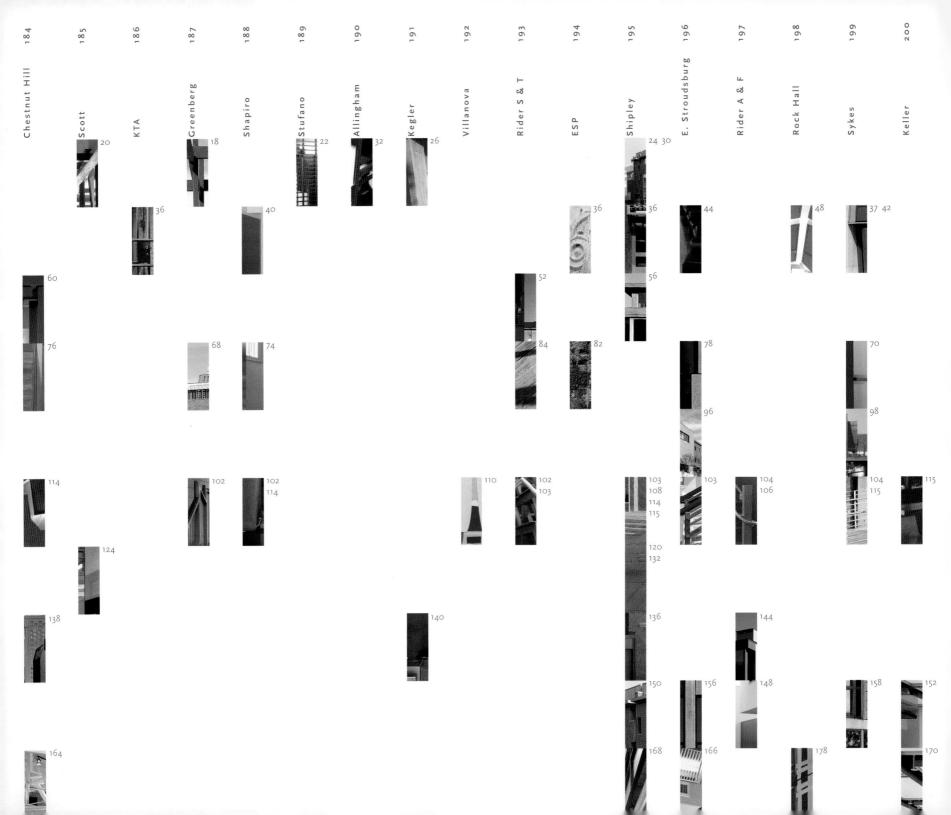

14 16
37 37
37
46
28
38
54 62
58
64
72
80
94
88 90
92
112 104
105
115
105 105 105
118
130 128
122
126
142
154
180
172 174 162 176

CONTENTS

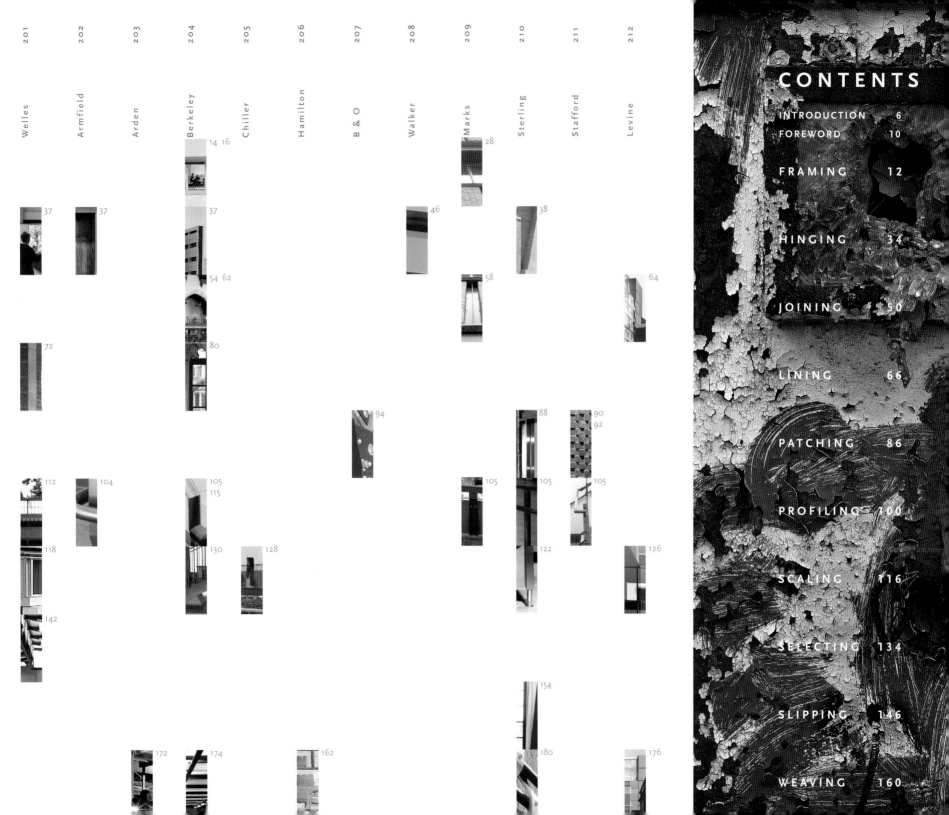

ARCHITECTURE AS PROCESS

In a world absorbed by images, the practice of Stephen Kieran and James Timberlake is exceptional indeed. For more than fifteen years, their patient commitment to the process of making has resulted in a true alternative to the notion of architecture as a final aesthetic product, which is common in conventional architectural practices, often oriented toward marketing an image or style. While most contemporary architects design buildings to be objectified as photogenic products aimed at critics or patrons in search of acclaim or corporate recognition, Kieran and Timberlake engage their clients in a process of discovery that is never preempted by some image of a future building. Each project is therefore unlike any other, not only embodying the clients' original aspirations but also, through the very process, encouraging the client to recognize the possible contributions the architecture might make to the social contract, to the making of places conducive to participation and reverie, and to the realization of the spiritual potential of human beings.

KieranTimberlake's technical processes are the result of close collaborations celebrating thoughtful making at many levels, which range from the work of craftsmen and fabricators to the productions of industrial manufacturers. Rejecting the notion of a preconceived, recognizable image of the office, KieranTimberlake produce work that is instead a thoughtful, meditative exploration of the possibilities of building technology.

Technology and techne-poiesis Technology confronts architecture with very complex problems, often expecting it to become a mere reflection of mindless processes or even to abdicate its expressive capacity in favor of some promised utopian efficiency or comfort. In the quest for an ethical architectural practice, it is never merely a question of either accepting or rejecting the technological world. We are all in our

flesh part of this technological world while we are called to be critical and aware of the dangers of technology as a mind-set. Conscious of the critical debate surrounding this issue, from the now classical works of Martin Heidegger to the works of more recent interpreters such as Gianni Vattimo, KieranTimberlake have chosen to become architect-builders. They engage to the fullest the possibilities of contemporary technology, pushing it through invention and imagination, while remaining profoundly respectful of historical values and mindful of the original sense of wonder. Over and beyond pragmatic issues, that original sense of wonder has always been the main attribute of the architect's technical productions.

This is a dangerous project, one that may easily be misinterpreted as the expression of a simplistic technological or formal interest. Yet KieranTimberlake's technical interests are rooted in history (that is, in what the philosopher Edmund Husserl termed "the spiritual history of Europe"). Their projects are evocative of the remarkably diverse works of craftsmanship and construction of Daedalus, that mythical first architect-inventor, in that their carefully assembled constructions are capable of seduction and even deception. These are ethically ambivalent productions, which can reveal the order of human destiny and its mixture of mortality and divinity.

The Client   During the Renaissance, Antonio Averlino "Il Filarete," like other writers on architecture of the time, was keenly aware that buildings have a life like animals or human beings. Buildings literally have to be born, and according to him, architect and client join in an intimate relationship. The architect, like a mother, receives a seed given by the client, like a father, and carries this germ of a building during nine months of careful gestation, indeed with no preconceptions other than dreams and shadowy images until the building becomes real. Once born, a building has to be cared for in good health, although, as Filarete recognized, it decays necessarily and eventually dies.

Clients play an important role in KieranTimberlake's practice. The work is collaborative, and clients are invited to participate in a process of discovery. This way of working is not easy and demands much good faith, even love, from both parties. The practice has fine-tuned the tactics it uses to define the programs of each project, mindful of the importance of programming in the act of making meaningful buildings that shape our lives and dreams.

History   Much of KieranTimberlake's practice deals with existing architectural fabric, which is the situation facing architects working in the developed world and now motivated by the growing concern for sustainable design. Explicitly questioning the modern fixation on eternity, KieranTimberlake, like Filarete, acknowledge the mortality of technological artifacts. The operations to which existing structures are subjected, described by the gerund forms in *Manual*, recognize that buildings have a life. These operations also engage the past without false pretensions, using history as Nietzsche called for it to be used: to enhance our present life and the creativity of future generations, rather than merely to glorify the past as a heavy burden that one would rather shed.

Manual   This book exemplifies a meditative process in which theories become posteriori tactics for construction. The gerunds describe processes that are engaged by various buildings, and the book recognizes that the issue is not to provide pictures and descriptions that might perpetuate the delusion that architecture can be experienced in any way other than by living it.

As knowledge and theories are discovered in the process of making, an intense alertness is demanded in order to identify the spark that can then be elaborated as a poetic strategy. This process is typical of the Aristotelian approach, in which appropriate categories are discovered empirically and evolve from the bottom up, as opposed to the Platonic approach, in which production is dominated by preconceived ideas that supposedly guarantee an ideal efficient or aesthetic result. The manual is paradoxical like those wonderful technical books of the late eighteenth century that documented technical prowess (such as J.R. Perronet's *Description des projets et de la construction des ponts*, Paris, 1782) while emphatically denying the possibility of providing a recipe or prescription for construction that could be universally applied. In this sense, KieranTimberlake's theories, lessons, and working drawings are an implicit critique of prescriptive or reductive practices in architecture. These range from the more traditional ways of working inherited from the nineteenth century [Ecole Polytechnique] to the contemporary planner's obsession with predictive knowledge (*savoir pour prévoir*). It is also a method at odds with most twentieth century avant-gardes and their blind faith in the predictive capacities of computers, either as tools of representation or as generators of formal modeling and fabrication.

Manual, finally, is about a particular way of teaching and learning, a particular experience that the practice is now in a position to share with others. This catalog of useful tactics for practice is the result of a collaborative project carried on by the office since its inception. Here again a precedent may be found in traditional apprenticeship and the responsibility that senior architects always accepted for the education of younger members of their profession. As in premodern practices, the senior partners of KieranTimberlake understand their responsibility to train and educate, that architecture is not merely learned in school. This is not because academic programs are necessarily defective but because the very assumptions underlying the relation between thinking and making are derived from a faulty model, which assumes that the only proper theory is a Platonic applied science. The processes of teaching and learning in the KieranTimberlake office are a mutually enriching experience for all involved. While a number of small offices do undertake the process successfully, engaging in the ethical responsibility at the scale of Kieran Timberlake is truly unusual. To place human values—the education and growth of future architects, life, and the human spirit—ahead of fashionable products, personal vanity, or fame is a courageous way of working, one that is fraught with dangers and that sometimes raises more questions than it is capable of answering.

Alberto Pérez-Gómez
Montreal, Canada

FOREWORD

Architecture is formed with materials; ideas are formed with words. Our physical response to architecture—once formed into structure—inevitably invites reflection. We turn to words to shape our reflection, continually circling through the domains of tangible and mental constructs, from the stuff of architecture to the words we use to grasp its intent. What follows is a way of thinking about architecture based on encounters. Like the structures it reflects, the text is itself episodic, by its very nature an incomplete, open-ended venture. Work provokes responses and questions. In response to the work, we form questions into words in our minds. Without words, we have no questions, merely latent consciousness. Without the work, we have, of course, no response leading us to questions and to active consciousness. The text in hand is a reification of reflections on our work that moves from architectural to verbal composition. We work, then reflect; then follows more work and further reflection. The value in the reflection is measured by the provocation it affords each new building.

Ten gerunds support our thesis. Gerunds—a protean part of speech upon which to structure reflections on building—are ambiguous, being both noun and verb. They suggest a world formed yet forming, still reaching beyond itself. The static noun element of each gerund is stable, while the dynamic verb element conveys process, the idea of a thing not yet completed. Depending upon context, each gerund moves back and forth between noun and verb, between building block and action. Gerunds are at once simple and complex, focused and diffuse. Aspects of buildings are similarly compound, with the whole and even single details inherent in several gerunds.

Manual refers to something done by hand or to a written set of instructions. Each of our ten gerunds relies on both these basic meanings of the word. Hand and craft are bound together. Hand is about making, and craft is about skill and tradition in making. Eventually, continuity of craft is assured as knowledge about making by hand and is recorded in a small book: a manual. The manual, then, is a handy set of directions intended to inform and clarify assemblage, a handbook. In our text, both uses of manual are joined in reflections on architecture at the beginning of the twenty-first century. Each of our ten gerunds—framing, hinging, joining, lining, patching, profiling, scaling, selecting, slipping, weaving—looks backward to the ancient craft origins of architecture and forward to an ever expanding universe of contemporary technology and architectural composition. They apply to artifacts of many types—container, clothing, building— but all begin with making, with the bringing together of materials to serve a common purpose: support, enclosure, aperture. All also reach beyond shelter and technique and toward organization, proportion, and placement—in a word, composition. We use these gerunds nearly every day with perfect confidence that we understand what they are all about, yet they all spring from so far below the surface of consciousness, from so close to their originating substance, that they rarely rise to obtrude themselves on the mind for critical reflection. Each gerund is a word used to convey a larger idea, but the import of the words themselves often lies hidden, submerged in the obscurity of a film of familiarity.

The origins of architecture are inherent in the conjunction of building crafts and materials science. The crafts are the stable foundations of the gerunds described here—the nouns. They connect us to building at the beginning of the path to architecture. Each gerund devolves as verb—an act spiraling outward from craft origin to building composition. Each moves outward from detail of construction to organization within the building, to position in the site.

The technology and composition of gerunds are dynamic, advancing—if intermittently—through work and reflection. One craft artifact may be replicated thousands of times with little alteration while in another artifact, innovation may be swift, bringing stunning change from one generation of artifact to the next. The change comes through learning derived from technology and composition. The materials architects use to make things also change, since such materials are inherently mutable. Evolution in materials gives rise to the potential for change in craft, to alteration and improvement in assembly. Evolution in assembly, in turn, suggests new prospects for composition, since in architecture, technology and composition are forever linked as omnipresent aspects of making. To make an artifact requires conscious choice, and no artifact is formed without some degree of both aesthetic and technical intent. You cannot have composition without a tradition of assembly. The only question is the degree of consciousness underlying the intent: less with successive, vernacular replication; more with custom, one-of-a-kind artifacts.

While the organization of material on a small scale has always been the province of craft, the conflation of craft with a contemporary usage of these gerunds expands its conventional realm of influence from small to large scale. The placement of a building, for example, can be just as much an act of craft as the organization of material is in creating a tapestry. The gerunds discussed here participate in a thoroughly classical dialectic that relates the detail to the whole. The detail is the seed that germinates in the handcraft and expands to inform the rationale for building placement. Conversely, one may read backward from placement to the originating craft code, locating the architectural genetics embedded in the relations among building materials. A catalog of gerunds is, of course, never complete but expands with each successive encounter. In this regard, gerunds as craft thrust beyond the orbit of normative traditions to a whole that implies an eternally expanding craft universe of material and assembly.

What does this manner of working mean to us and to those who work with us? What is it like to be in our shop, to make buildings and places with few preconceptions of material, structure, or plan, and to set to work with no single illuminating image to rely on? It would be far less demanding for architect and client alike if we chose to see the end product before setting out. Many, in fact, prefer to take a path that leads directly, inevitably to a prefigured ideal outcome that is known and approved at the outset. Instead, we choose a process crafted for each episodic journey toward a no less inevitable—if unknown—future. We seek to discover the inherent beauty and characteristics locked within each project. This can be an arduous process, yet for those who elect the journey, whether collaborators in our shop or our client participants, the depth of our collective vision is far richer at the conclusion than at the beginning.

Stephen Kieran and James Timberlake
Philadelphia, Pennsylvania

FRAMING

Berkeley

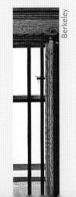

Berkeley

Greenberg

Scott

Stufano

Shipley

Kegler

Marks

Framing is in essence the visualization of invisible yet empirically known forces described by the science of statics and the aesthetics of vision. These forces align materials in two ways: scientifically, as armature about which floors, walls, and roofs array themselves to form shelter; and aesthetically, as emphasis that focuses vision on prospects in the world beyond.

Framing allows architecture to exist. It is the precursor, the enabling actor, a force field within which other acts of building array themselves. Without framing we would have no buildings of size or complexity. Without framing, architecture would have begun and ended with the man-made cave, the domed hut made entirely of stone, earth, or ice. Framing is to architecture what gravity is to the solar system. It is the action-of-force that orders the materials that form architecture. Just as an intellectual position or argument requires framing for comprehension, most buildings require a support, a framework about which the materials and forces of architecture can draw themselves into effective order.

Ultimately, framing is expressed by material, but in its conception, it is an action. It is supporting, not a thing itself but an abstraction that, like gravity, focuses and limits our area of vision as well as our potential realm of enclosure. Building materials in themselves have little inherent organization without the discipline of framing. As a construct of the mind, architectural framing is a set of countervailing vectors. It is a field of paired forces in balance, one force moving down or out, seeking earth, and its counterpart moving up or in, seeking the sky. Fortunately, the science of statics charts the ways whereby neither will succeed, for the desired result is a draw that etches a new realm of enclosure between earth and sky. Framing negotiates the conflict between the limitations of the materials of the enclosing membrane—be it floor, wall, or roof—and the

desire for a purposeful void within. The materials are limited in size by custom, physical properties, and the facts of production. Typically, the desired span of a space is greater than the size and capacity of any single member of the enclosing materials. The characteristics of framing—size, proportion, spacing, and configuration—are most often a function of the span of the desired void, its external and internal loads, and the strength and spanning capacity of the materials selected to enclose the space. The ordering of the architecture we seek derives in large measure from the creative manipulation of the limitations of materials through the medium of framing.

Once secure within the enclosure the frame enables, we are then fascinated by its opposite: the portal—the window or door that leads from within to without. The allure of the opening is embedded in its contradiction of the wall. Without the prospect of connection, we cannot understand separation. Without a wall to separate, there is no mystery beyond what lures us to seek a portal. Without a portal, there is no complement, no breach that adds freedom to security. The paradox of enclosure is that once created through separation, it invites connection. If the purpose of the wall is to keep outside out, then the door and the window exist to let limited aspects of the outside in. Framing mediates connection and separation.

Framing is an enabler, not an element of architecture. It exists for all of architecture but itself. Framing begins and ends as a construct in the mind and eye and is more force than material presence.

FRAMING

Berkeley   Medieval architecture is about torture—the more pushing and shoving the better. You take what the wall gives you, but you can also go mad banging your head against that same wall. Sometimes solutions come more easily on their own. The prospect and the desire for this portal occurred during a trip to Italy. During the bid/negotiation process we discovered that the new window could be concealed within the frame of an existing wood panel in the adjacent dining hall. The resulting abstractions are more medieval at their core than the 1920s revival architecture on the rest of Yale's campus. The portal, cut into a thick wall, begins a conversation with the dining hall and its new balcony beyond.

The construction manager saved this cut until the very last, hoping it would just go away or that the owner would not approve the change order. He couldn't bear the idea of cutting the existing wood paneling.

CF.   16 37 54 62 80 105 115 130 174

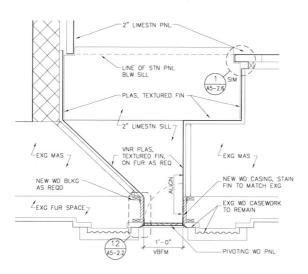

WINDOW PLAN

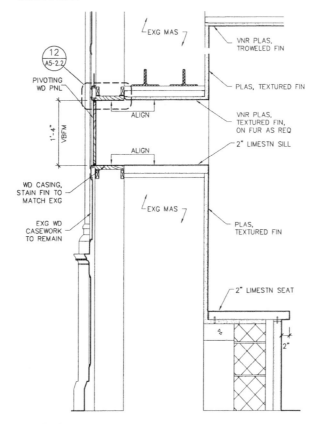

WINDOW SECTION

MASTERS of COLLEGE
CHARLES SEYMOUR
1934-1937
SAMUEL B. HEMINGWAY
1937-1950
THOMAS C. MENDENHALL II
1950-1959
CHARLES A. WALKER
1959-1969

FRAMING

Berkeley Few can resist peering through a little hole to a world beyond. The asymmetrical angling of these windows is a quiet abstraction of medieval architecture, which further emphasizes the wall depth and draws the body into the role of voyeur. Most of these framing moments were discovered incident by incident. At the stair that reaches up to the dining hall balcony, we wanted to create a more generous pause by pushing the landing into an existing phone booth and storeroom. By removing the wooden panels, James Gamble Rogers's elaborate wood carvings become transparent, and a more modern sense of public spatial depth is infused into formerly introverted rooms. At the bottom of the stair, a body-size hole into the multipurpose room extends the view through that space into the activity of the hall beyond, which continues the dialogue of circumstantial viewing.

CF.   14 37 54 62 80 105 115 130 174

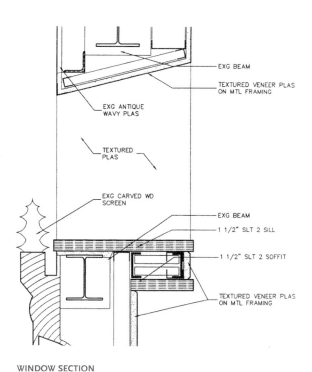

EXG BEAM

TEXTURED VENEER PLAS ON MTL FRAMING

EXG ANTIQUE WAVY PLAS

TEXTURED PLAS

EXG CARVED WD SCREEN

EXG BEAM

1 1/2" SLT 2 SILL

1 1/2" SLT 2 SOFFIT

TEXTURED VENEER PLAS ON MTL FRAMING

WINDOW SECTION

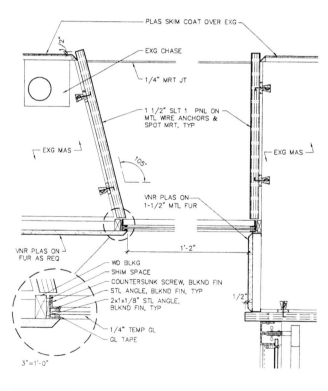

PLAS SKIM COAT OVER EXG

EXG CHASE

1/4" MRT JT

1 1/2" SLT 1 PNL ON
MTL WIRE ANCHORS &
SPOT MRT, TYP

EXG MAS

EXG MAS

105°

VNR PLAS ON
1-1/2" MTL FUR

1'-2"

VNR PLAS ON
FUR AS REQ

WD BLKG
SHIM SPACE
COUNTERSUNK SCREW, BLKND FIN
STL ANGLE, BLKND FIN, TYP
2x1x1/8" STL ANGLE,
BLKND FIN, TYP

1/2"

1/4" TEMP GL
GL TAPE

3"=1'-0"

WINDOW PLAN

17

FRAMING

Greenberg Views resonate through the house from front to back, breaching the meadow edge. While the house and the thicket bracket the landscape at the exterior, moments of symmetrically framed views from the interior penetrate through the house to the landscape beyond. The sky becomes prominent without the congestion of neighbors. A piece of its unimaginable volume is captured for contemplation by a frame above the skylight of the drawing studio.

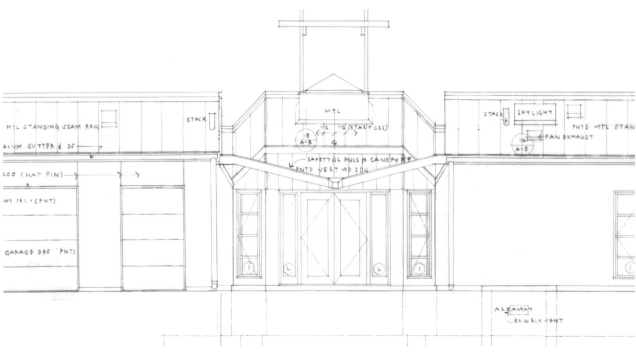

CF. 68 102

STUDIO ELEVATION

FRAMING

Scott The townhouse was ordinary: a central stair with rooms to the front and rear. Our intention was to transform what was potentially extraordinary—a four-story stair shaft—into the project anchor. Enhancing this verticality by framing it with spiraling glass guards and wooden handrails, we created a focus for the placeless rooms of the existing house. While the frame is a fictive moment wrapped around a real column (the stair), the wood and glass frames operate at a programmatic level as well: they present degrees of privacy or community from one floor to the next by offering the opportunity to separate or open adjoining spaces to the stair.

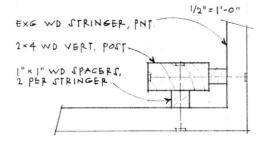

STRINGER DETAIL

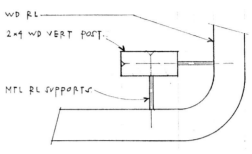

RAILING DETAIL

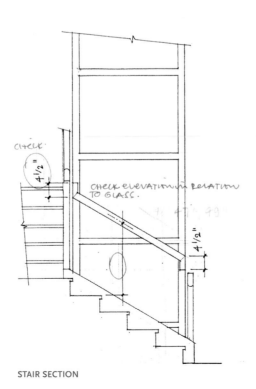

STAIR SECTION

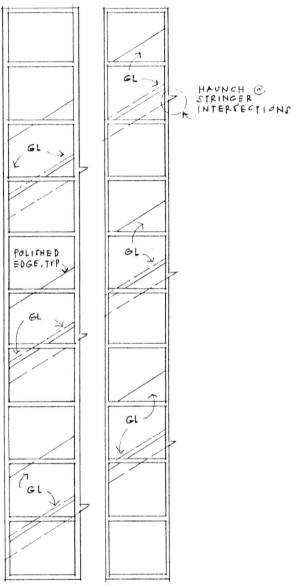

HAUNCH @
STRINGER
INTERSECTIONS

GL

GL

POLISHED
EDGE, TYP

GL

GL

GL

GL

GL

TYPICAL FRAME ELEVATION

21

FRAMING

Stufano   A frame is needed to construct a tapestry. Remove it, and the fabric remains. In architecture, the frame stays as permanent armature. Brick piers operate as a subtext to the order of the weave by grounding the spaces with massive swaths of program and circulation that extend through the house. The program is framed internally by the construction of the rooms as zones of space and of those zones as extensions into the landscape.

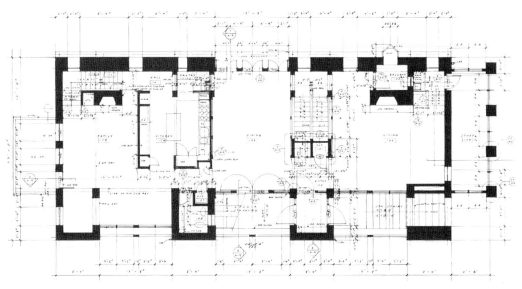

FIRST FLOOR PLAN

FRAMING

Shipley Slate is most often used as a roofing material. Here we inverted its usual position by hanging slate on the walls. The structure is composed of transverse-bearing walls, which leaves the long exterior walls as infill-spatial enclosures. We thought immediately of roof sheathing as a contrast to the masonry-bearing walls. To help convince the trustees, the head-master came back from a trip to Vermont with photos of farmhouses using a similar detail. Our favorite moments tend to be in the circumstantial nature of construction; here the scaffold erected by the contractor becomes a means of construction in dialogue with an intention: a framing of the frame.

Lead-coated copper flashings frame slate panels, allowing air movement behind the exterior finish while preventing water infiltration and protecting the unfinished edge of the slate.

CF. 30 36 56 103 108 114 115 120 132
136 150 168

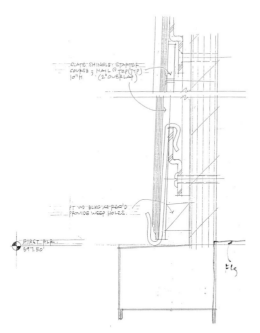

WINDOW-HEAD SECTION

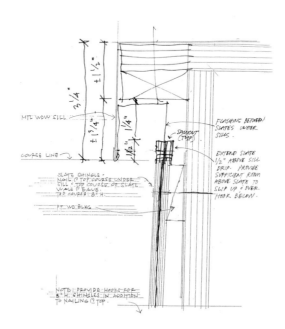

WINDOWSILL SECTION

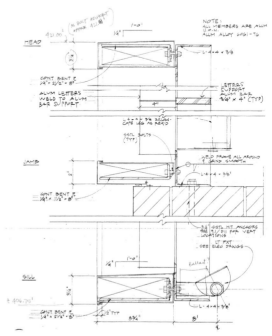

ENTRY SIGN SECTION

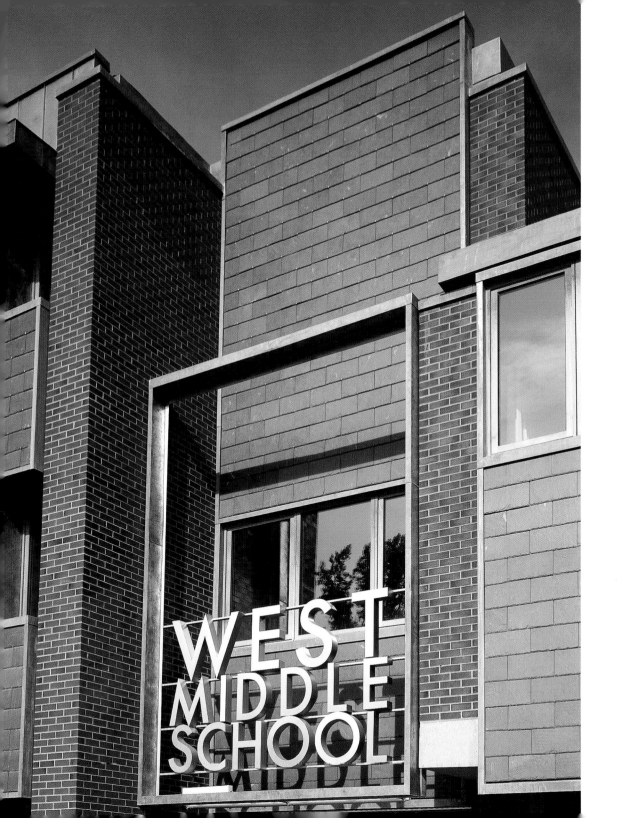

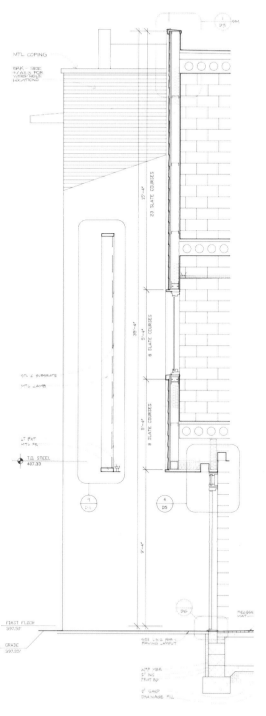

ENTRY SIGN–WALL SECTION

FRAMING

Kegler The existing structure is a wood-frame and board-sheathed shed. Our strategy was to invert the existing enclosure with the addition. From the outside, the addition is an elemental lean-to with a shed roof and supporting structure; on the inside, a second internal glass frame is misaligned with the columns. While the frame is concealed in the existing shed, it is revealed by the new roof. The lap pool participates through reflections, that transfer the image of the frame on the water.

POOL HOUSE SECTION

CF. 140

FRAMING

Marks Prior to Marks, all of our masonry walls either bore the building structure or were self-bearing and restrained by the building structure. Marks was the first time we hung a masonry wall from a steel frame. Relieving angles stratify the walls horizontally. Vertical rips were introduced, centered on windows, both to introduce air to the pressure-equalized chambers behind the panels and to provide for lateral expansion. The result is a two-dimensional framing of wall panels that parallels the three-dimensional structural framing of columns and beams. The bounding of relatively small brick panels required careful layout and spacing by the masonry contractor.

Masonry structures over three stories require relieving angles at every floor to bear the brick or stone façade.

CF. 58 105

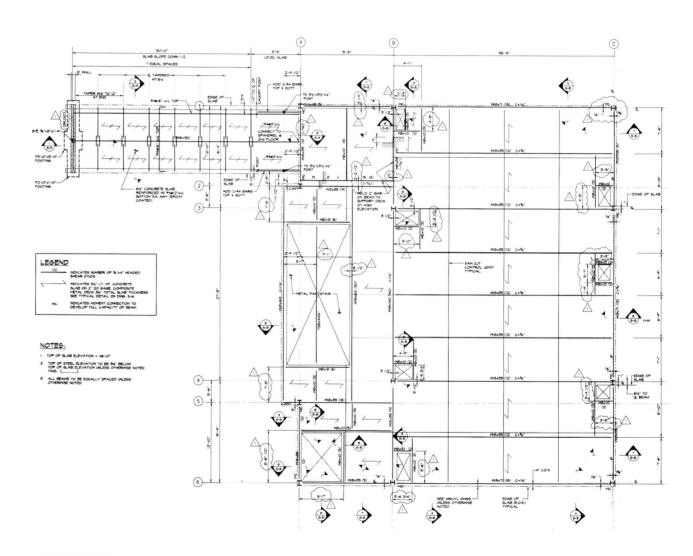

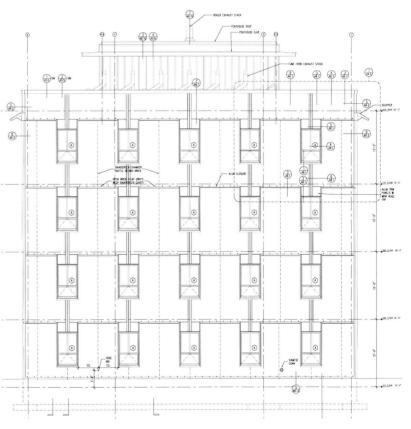

EAST ELEVATION

29

FRAMING

Shipley Previously a placeless field, the new school building acts as a frame defining the edge of a campus commons to the west. By slightly inflecting the simple bar, directionality is introduced and a double-faced space with defined programs is formed. The new entry focuses on an existing carriage house, with the middle school flanking and framing one side. To the rear, the framing is both toward and away from the existing buildings, forming space for play.

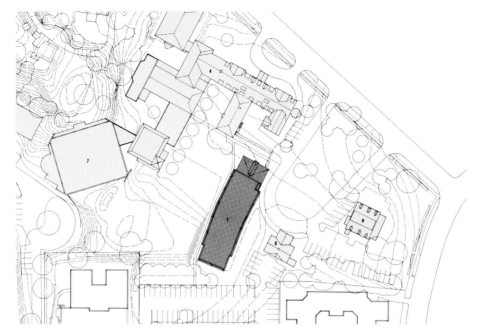

SITE PLAN

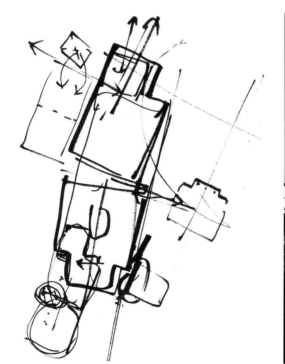

CF.   24 36 56 103 108 114 115 120 132
      136 150 168

30

FRAMING

Allingham Driving through Maryland's Eastern shore on our way to the site, we saw many drying sheds. While this house derives from these sheds and other local styles, it was a seminal project for us in that the primary issue was the depth (literal and figurative) of the frame. The frame is a passage for utilities and a marker of view and landscape, as well as a program organizer. This house was never built.

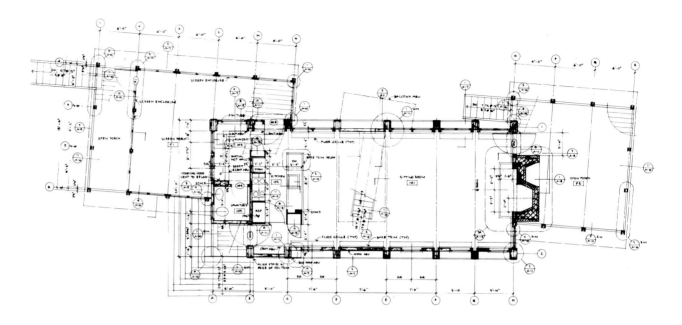

FIRST FLOOR PLAN

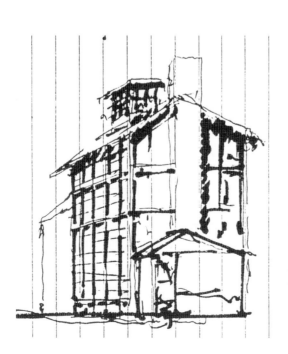

HINGING

Berkeley

Sterling

Shapiro

Sykes

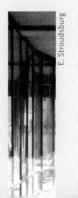
E. Stroudsburg

Walker

Just as the word *hinging* embodies opposing notions of arrest and movement, so too does it imply the opposing states of open and closed. Hinging came into existence to allow architecture antithetical desires: access and security, revelation and privacy, connection and containment. We know hinging in its craft origin as a literal mechanical device. Today, in the form of fixed hinging, it is a figurative compositional strategy to adjust and open.

The wall came into existence to separate interior from exterior, to secure an inner world from the unwanted intrusion of temperature, moisture, and predator. The framed or arched portal was certainly part of this first wall, allowing passage between the newly formed interior world and the exterior world from which it was recently cleaved. The desire for selective exclusion and inclusion, and for reversible exclusion and inclusion, could not have come long after the original desire for an enclosing wall. It is this desire for selective passage, for closed and open space, that gives rise to hinging that allows alteration between arrest and movement. As a contrivance to effect selection and alteration of position, hinging was the first mechanism—as opposed to element—of architecture. Mechanical hinging is a device, occasionally continuous but more often intermittent, that enables a portion of a wall to open and close. Prior to hinging, architecture was largely an affair of static elements: columns, beams, rafters, and walls were and remain among those elements. Now called "hardware," the mechanical hinge is the enabler of change, the device that realizes a dynamic rather than a static relation between adjoining spaces.

In an extension of this potential for change, fixed hinging is also a strategy of composition. It is a formal tactic that regulates, beyond literal movement, some discontinuity or change in plane at the moments of conception and eventual construction. The development of fixed hinging largely parallels that of mechanical hinging. Just as mechanical hinging effects change to accommodate the opposing states of open and closed, fixed hinging adjusts the inherently static artifacts of architecture to place and purpose. The desire to adjust planarity purposefully once and then to fix it during design and construction derives most often from a comprehensive sense of position relative to place. Through fixed hinging, walls and ceilings can overcome their inherently static nature to order themselves dynamically. Hinging can, for example, purposefully order a set of broken ceiling planes so that each aligns itself differentially to enhance acoustical clarity. Or hinging can pivot a wall, panel by panel, to rotate a building in response to its site. Sectionally, hinging can adjust walls vertically, ordering changes in the inclination of planes.

Neither solely static element nor solely dynamic mechanism, hinging is the ultimate gerund in that it accommodates both arrest and movement. Just as the physically reversing mechanism of literal hinging overcame the static nature of the enclosing wall, so too does figurative hinging, which is a conceptual artifice of adjustment, enliven site and use, which are the more static elements of architecture.

Rock Hall

35

HINGING

Normally a door has the primary function of protecting an enclosed space from undesirable access. The door is also traditionally viewed as a symbolical passage, interrupting the continuity of the surrounding walls. It is our impression that architects today are less likely to consider this last point. Instead, they tend to focus on the door's functional characteristics. Doors are crucial elements in a building. They negotiate the delicate transition between outside and inside, to the extent that the door closes a wall's opening; it is simultaneously the continuation of this wall and its most vulnerable point. A door is a site of particular tension and as such it should be studied, designed, and experienced.

Painted steel and glass, painted wood, mahogany and glass, mahogany, teak, oak, wood lattice and mirrored glass.

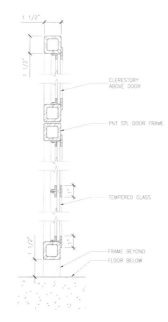

CLERESTORY ABOVE DOOR

PNT STL DOOR FRAME

TEMPERED GLASS

FRAME BEYOND
FLOOR BELOW

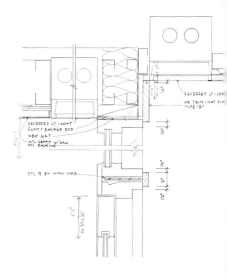

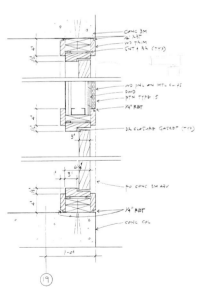
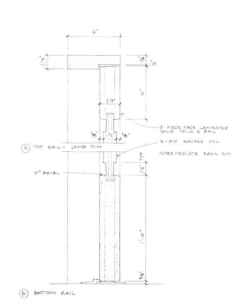
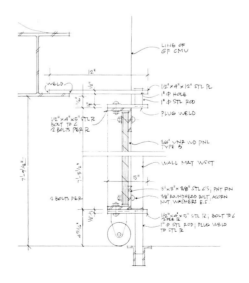
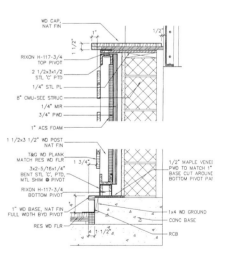

HINGING

Sterling No less than thirteen drawings were required to dissect this wall's twenty-eight-foot length. Much of it had to come down and be reset when it was not properly understood. The pointing was especially difficult to achieve; the contrast between the flat recessed ashlar joint and the flush limestone joint, so necessary to the overall depth, required numerous trials.

There were days when the masons constructing this wall made little effort to conceal their disdain for us and for it. Yet there was the day when one of them sought us out to say how beautiful the wall was and that he had taken home to his children a photograph of the almost finished wall. Visiting the site several weeks after accepting the final stonework, we found the master mason again reworking the joints.

CF. 88 105 122 154 180

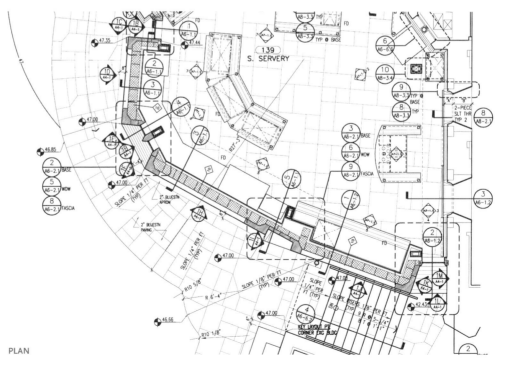

PLAN

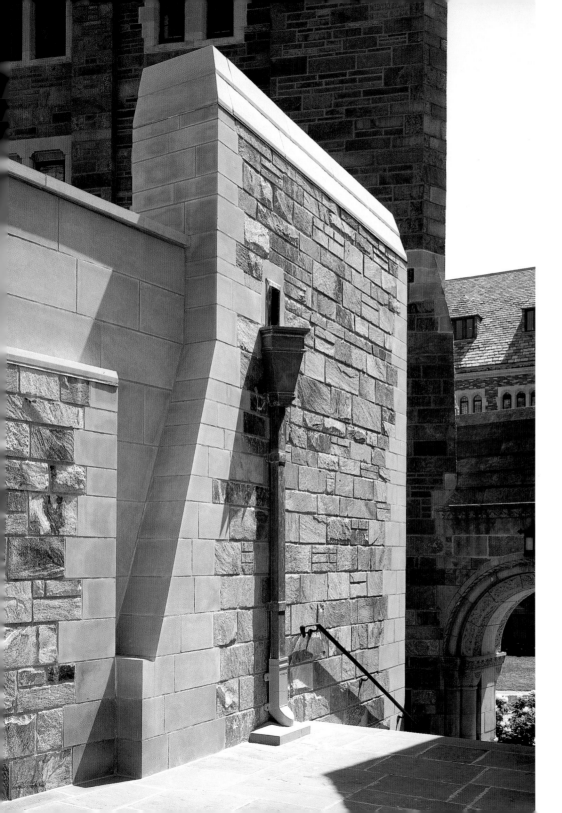

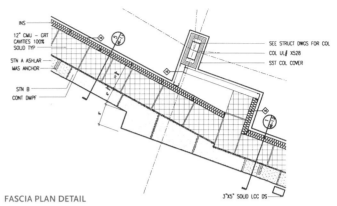

FASCIA PLAN DETAIL

Labels on diagram:
INS
12" CMU – GRT CAVITIES 100% SOLID TYP
STN A ASHLAR MAS ANCHOR
STN B
CONT DMPF
SEE STRUCT DWGS FOR COL
COL UL# X528
SST COL COVER
3"X5" SOLID LCC DS

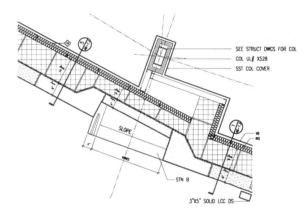

SLOT PLAN DETAIL

Labels on diagram:
SEE STRUCT DWGS FOR COL
COL UL# X528
SST COL COVER
SLOPE
STN B
3"X5" SOLID LCC DS

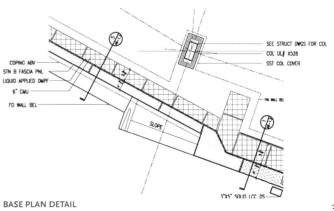

BASE PLAN DETAIL

Labels on diagram:
COPING ABV
STN B FASCIA PNL
LIQUID APPLIED DMPF
6" CMU
FO WALL BEL
SEE STRUCT DWGS FOR COL
COL UL# X528
SST COL COVER
FW WALL BEL
SLOPE
3"X5" SOLID LCC DS

HINGING

Shapiro   Not even an open field is more placeless than the typical American subdivision. How do you ground the house within such circumstances? Ironically, embracing the geometry of the developer's site plan by hinging the house on the curve of the street becomes a subversion of the suburb even as it anchors the house within its context. This act of place making continues at multiple scales within the house. The windows are creased to negotiate the bending, the garage hinged to open a car court. Additionally, the hinge at the back side of the house grounds the project to its site and focuses the view toward the spaces between the backyards of all the homes along the block.

CF. 74 102 114

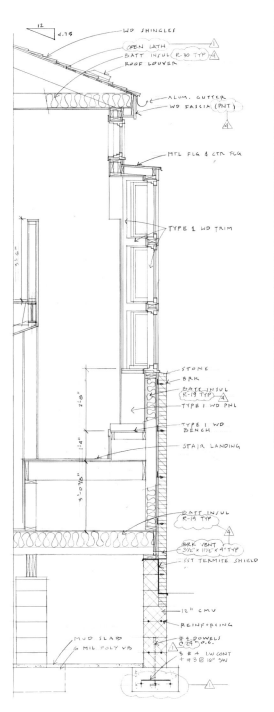

STAIR WINDOW SECTION

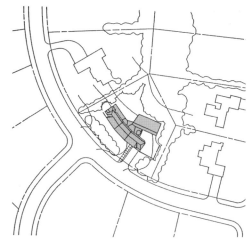

SITE PLAN

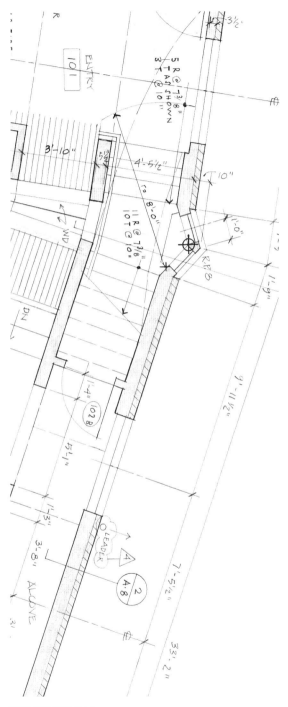

STAIR WINDOW PLAN

HINGING

Sykes The plan derives from a radial pivot about the central column or pin. We were probably too restrained in the treatment of the column. Volumetrically, it is an effective way of making the space important, but its connection to the orthogonal structural system of the rest of the building is underdetailed. The exterior wall section hinges at the top, lifting up and out at the bottom to reveal both the inside and outside of the structure. The exterior shingled wall above laps the glass wall below, with a steel tube as an intermediate hinge that connects the upper and lower panels.

CF. 37 70 98 104 115 158

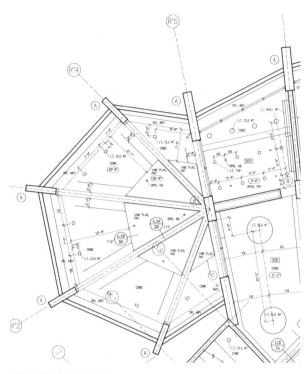

REFLECTED CEILING PLAN

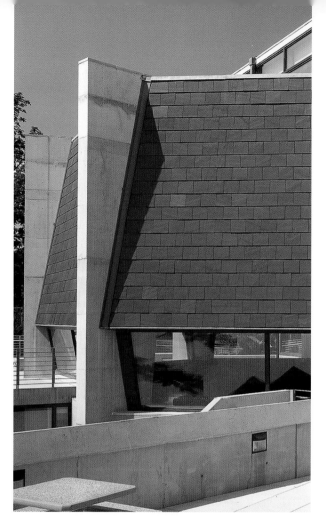

42

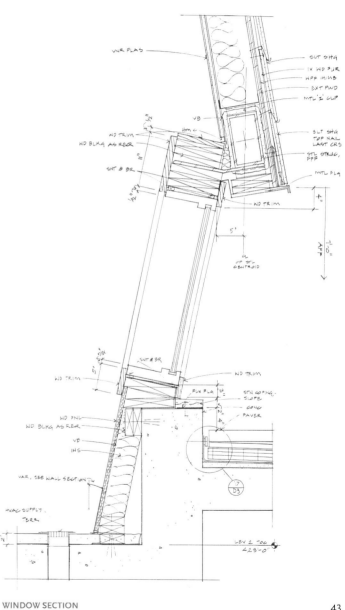

WINDOW SECTION

HINGING

E. Stroudsburg   Cracking the wall in plan fuses a social intention with a formal one by turning a solitary space of passage into an inflected invitation to socialize. The concave bend of the wall organizes the seating for crossing views on passersby and the courtyard beyond. Not only can one watch the passerby on the sidewalk, but the viewer can also easily watch others watching. The pivot point is inferred, between butt glazed glass panes.

CF.   78 96 103 156 166

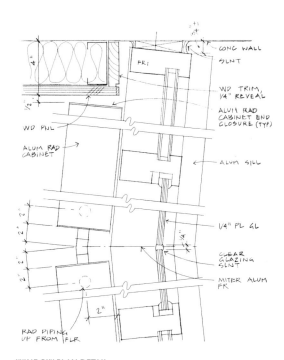

WINDOW PLAN DETAIL

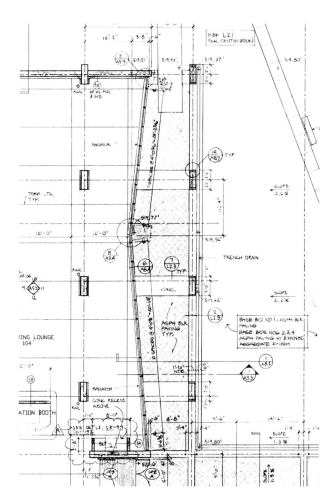

LOBBY WINDOW PLAN

HINGING

Walker   Inflecting the ceiling provides visual and acoustic relief and focuses attention on the performer. Operable wooden acoustic panels in the wall also participate in the hinging dialogue by swinging open or shut as a means of tuning the space. When the doors are open, the room absorbs sound; closing the doors creates a space more reflective of sound.

The wooden acoustic panels in the wall weigh a couple hundred pounds each. Finding a hinge that wasn't a heavy-duty floor mounted industrial hinge took us on quite a search. Few concealed casework-appropriate hinges are rated for that kind of load.

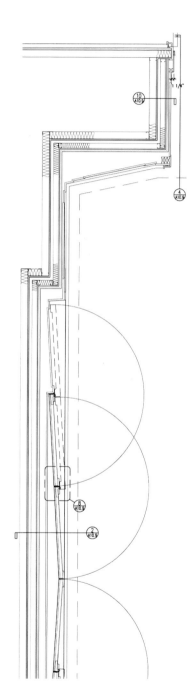

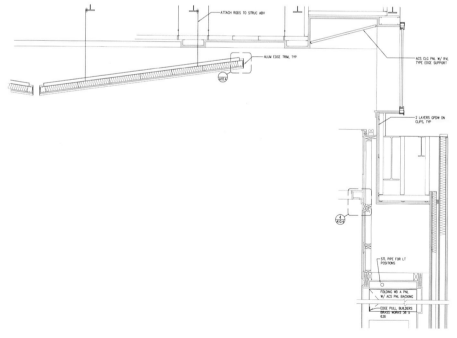

46   ACOUSTIC PANELS PLAN   CEILING SECTION

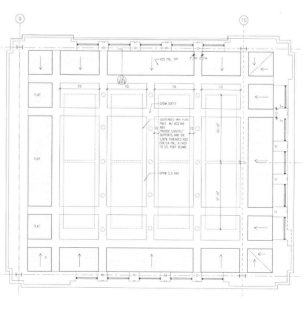

REFLECTED CEILING PLAN

HINGING

Rock Hall As part of a larger renovation, the new recital room was inserted into a structure that was once a synagogue. The movement of the ceiling transforms every surface in the room. The resultant hinge improves the acoustics and throttles the scale of the space to that of a private performance. The metal fin dividing the wood panels works in its oscillation between beauty and crudity. The volume of the original room reveals itself between the panels. These panels become a visual and acoustic foil to the rectangular room and scrim daylight within the existing volume.

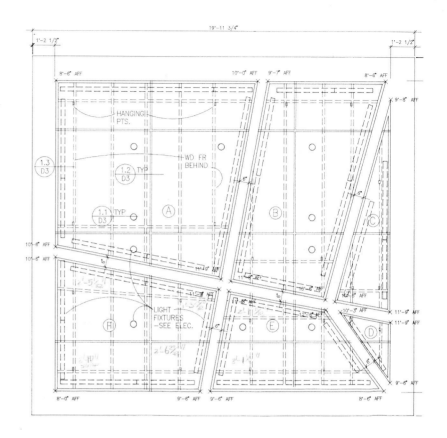

REFLECTED CEILING PLAN

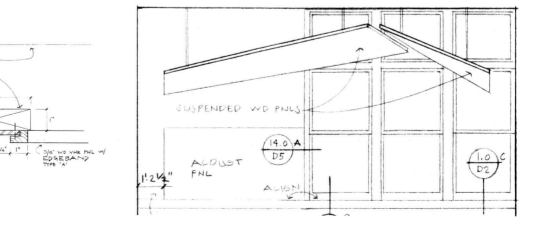

CEILING JOINT SECTION

INTERIOR ELEVATION

JOINING

Rider S & T

Berkeley

Shipley

Marks

Chestnut Hill

Berkeley

Joining is yoked to separating as open is to closed, as here is to there. The two are opposites whose meanings depend on each other. The desire to join owes its existence to the fact of separation: without separation, there is no need for joining; without joining, we cannot comprehend what it means to be separate. Separation in architecture arises from the characteristics of the materials to be assembled into a building or from the evolution of the site. Joining is the means by which we assemble building materials and buildings themselves into larger wholes.

In response to the logistics of construction and to the properties of materials that limit the size of any single construction member, two types of joint are available to expand its size: end joints and edge joints. End joints extend the length of a material by joining the end of one member to another, and edge joints extend the width of a material by joining one member along its length to the edge of another. Which of these two joints is selected depends on the purpose, the physical properties of the elements joined, the experience of the desired craftsman, and on the available tools and compositional preferences.

For example, even if we can roll a 500-foot-long steel beam, we cannot move it; and even if we could, it would be difficult to join it to other beams or materials so as to generate the requisite continuity and closure while allowing for thermal expansion and contraction along its length. End joints allow us to join steel beams of convenient size into as long a beam as we require.

Edge joints are useful in a different way. Walls cannot be constructed of unlimited length and height. Lateral movement in walls is countered by two types of joint: those that control, or that tell a wall where to crack; and those that free the wall to shrink and expand as it may. Vertically, masonry walls must be periodically supported by transferring the weight of the material

to a frame through structural relieving angles. The relieving angle is an omnipresent form of edge joint in tall masonry construction.

Joints are also used to effect a change in plane. Some materials, such as metals, can be rolled or extruded to change plane, but others, such as wood, cannot be folded without ripping the structure of the material apart. In a masonry wall, stone quoins at the corners where walls join are a form of dovetail joint, with the interlocking laps conceptually similar to the wooden dovetail common in handcrafted furniture. By contrast, in the pressure-equalized wall, the right-angle joint is a stopped lap that has air space at the corner, revealing the stratification of materials to be a new form of joining at changes in plane.

New things added to old things—be it a new building added to an older one or reinforcement added to a distressed truss—is another form of joining. New joints added to old allow artifacts developed at different times to exist in harmony and to move independently through expansion joints between existing structures and their additions. Circumstances on a site evolve over time often to generate separation. A campus expands to the other side of a road. The road becomes busy and is widened. Fences are added alongside to restrict crossing. Once a connector, the road is now a divider in need of a joint. As in its ancient craft origin, the joining born of separation is still a requirement of assembly; it is also a moment of illumination in the craft of the architect, as separation is transformed into union. The joint is invited, inevitable.

Levine

JOINING

Rider S & T   This was one of the few clients who did not tell us to get lost in the early years of our searching for projects. He held the philosophy that one receives better attention and work from someone who is on the way up than from someone who has already made it. After working on small renovation projects around the university, we were given our chance. Phase one of the project was dominated by labs and associated equipment arranged along a circulation spine perpendicular to the corridor of the existing building. This space was expressed in the stairs at each end of the building. The stair to the south provides a focal point for those on the academic quadrangle and a continuous reentry to the landscape for those inside the building as they move from floor to floor. A new cross-campus pedestrian walk replaces a service drive and joins the Science and Technology building to our new Admissions building on the opposite side of campus.

CF.   84 102 103

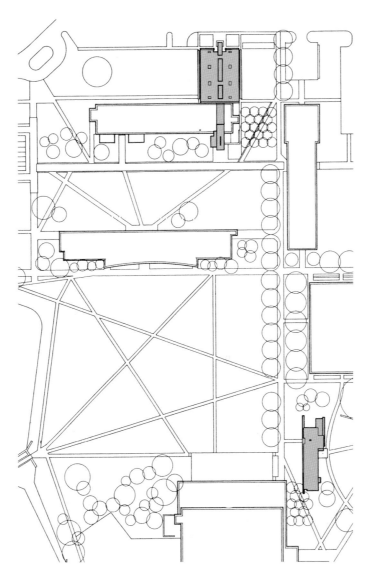

SITE PLAN

JOINING

Berkeley The new balcony is itself a joint, connecting the dining hall to the Swiss Room, which was previously accessible only from an adjoining exterior entryway. Originally the window and the wooden ceiling beams in this two-story alcove were way overhead. In an Alice-in-Wonderland twist, these high elements are now accessible, allowing for the experience of gothic architecture from a different perspective. The arched stone window heads are now at one's feet. The metal base was scaled to the size of the other existing details and functions as a lip to keep feet from going through the opening at the window and balcony guardrail.

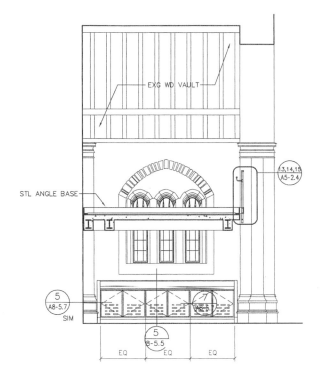

BALCONY TRANSVERSE SECTION

STL ANGLE BASE

EXG WD VAULT

13,14,15
A5-2.4

5
A8-5.7
SIM

5
8-5.5

EQ   EQ   EQ

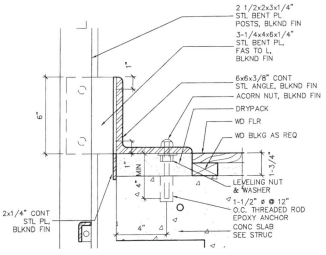

BASE/BALCONY-RAIL SECTION

2 1/2x2x3x1/4"
STL BENT PL
POSTS, BLKND FIN

3-1/4x4x6x1/4"
STL BENT PL,
FAS TO L,
BLKND FIN

6x6x3/8" CONT
STL ANGLE, BLKND FIN

ACORN NUT, BLKND FIN

DRYPACK

WD FLR

WD BLKG AS REQ

LEVELING NUT
& WASHER

1-1/2" ∅ @ 12"
O.C. THREADED ROD
EPOXY ANCHOR
CONC SLAB
SEE STRUC

2x1/4" CONT
STL PL,
BLKND FIN

CF.   14 16 37 62 80 105 115 130 174

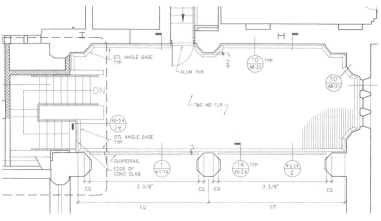

BALCONY PLAN

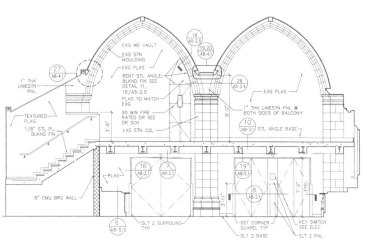

BALCONY SECTION

JOINING

Shipley   Our initial idea for this clerestory resembled a duck-tail airfoil to capture southern light. The client referenced a truck "sort of like the head end of a Kenworth," and we were sent back to the drawing board. Developing a profile that would provide both a head-on end and a front to the school entry drive took dozens of iterations. What was built is a modest hymn to the music-room program and to the building's head house condition, but we still refer to it as the cadaver table.

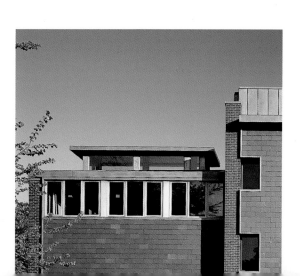

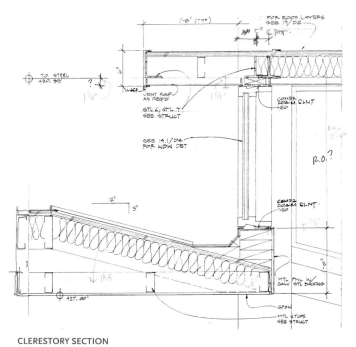

CLERESTORY SECTION

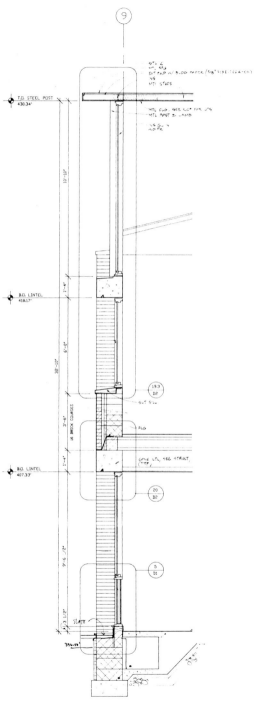

WALL SECTION

JOINING

Marks From a distance, the windows act as proportional joiners to the rest of campus. The opening size was arrived at through the combination of thirty-six inches of lab casework at the floor and the ceiling depth required by a modern laboratory. This combination gave us a dimension at odds with the rest of the campus, but by constructing a metal scrim at the window head, the apparent height of the opening was increased. Joining a window to a masonry wall is always an act of some compromise. The window is precise, while the masonry is inherently crude. Generally, the construction joint is closed with flexible sealants. Here, however, shadow, not material, becomes the joint between window and wall.

The pressure-equalized chamber behind the brick panels gives rise to an open joint between window jambs and masonry. The gap allows air to circulate freely behind the brick. The moisture that inevitably makes its way into the wall swiftly evaporates within this system.

CF. 28 105

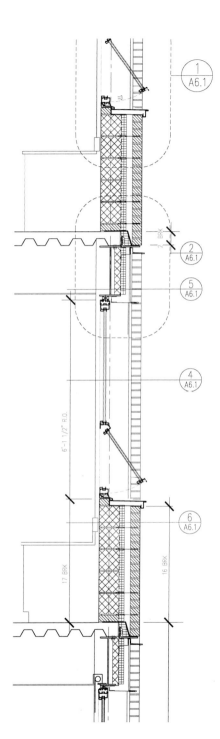

WALL SECTION

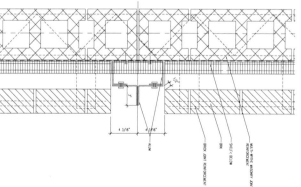

VERTICAL RAINSCREEN JOINT PLAN DETAIL

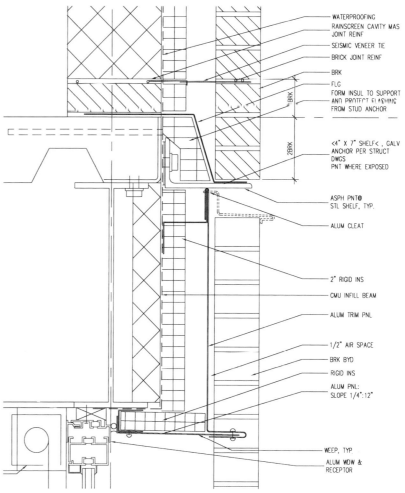

WATERPROOFING
RAINSCREEN CAVITY MAS JOINT REINF
SEISMIC VENEER TIE
BRICK JOINT REINF
BRK
FLG
FORM INSUL TO SUPPORT AND PROTECT FLASHING FROM STUD ANCHOR

BRK

2BRK

<4" X 7" SHELF< , GALV ANCHOR PER STRUCT DWGS
PNT WHERE EXPOSED

ASPH PNT@ STL SHELF, TYP.

ALUM CLEAT

2" RIGID INS

CMU INFILL BEAM

ALUM TRIM PNL

1/2" AIR SPACE

BRK BYD

RIGID INS

ALUM PNL: SLOPE 1/4":12"

WEEP, TYP

ALUM WDW & RECEPTOR

WINDOW-HEAD/METAL FASCIA SECTION

JOINING

Chestnut Hill A metal foot joins the jamb struts of the metal frames to the existing terrazzo floor. Reveals separate metal channels from the existing walls. Additional reveals segregate metal channels from plates and drywall. Joining is now a negative affair of shadow. The construction tolerances of the materials recede into shadow, appear in darkness and not covered over or capped. The reveals connect one joint to the next, completing a network of refined lines among the elements of the screen and providing a hint of the ceiling tracery in the activity room at the end of the corridor.

CF. 76 114 138 164

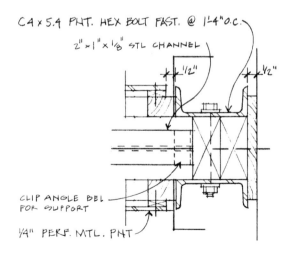

C 4 x 5.4 PNT. HEX BOLT FAST. @ 1'-4" O.C.

2" x 1" x ⅛" STL CHANNEL

½"   ½"

CLIP ANGLE BEL FOR SUPPORT

¼" PERF. MTL. PNT

JAMB/WALL-CONNECTION PLAN DETAIL

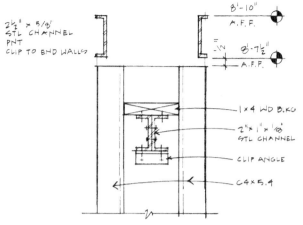

2½" × ⅝"
STL CHANNEL
PNT
CLIP TO END WALLS

8'-10"
A.F.F.

8'-7½"
A.F.F.

1×4 WD BLKG

2"×1"×⅛"
STL CHANNEL

CLIP ANGLE

C4×5.4

BEAM SECTION

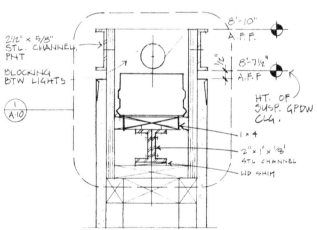

2½" × ⅝"
STL. CHANNEL,
PNT

BLOCKING
BTW LIGHTS

1
A·10

8'-10"
A.F.F.

8'-7½"
A.F.F.

HT. OF
SUSP. GPDW
CLG.

1 × 4

2"×1"×⅛"
STL CHANNEL

WD SHIM

BEAM SECTION WITH LIGHT RECESS

61.

JOINING

Berkeley   We were concerned that these portals might be overly aggressive, but the effect is quite a subtle leaking of the formerly hermetic library into the other shared building spaces. Connecting these spaces with slot windows allows the hidden basement library to be found and the buried basement hallway to be an event. When one is deep in study, a moment of respite can be found in the glancing views of passing figures.

The variety of materials in this detail led to some construction-sequencing difficulties. First the hole had to be cut in the brick then measured for the slate. After the slate was installed, measurements were taken for the blackened steel frame. Finally, after the steel was installed, the glass could be measured and cut. Nothing could be fabricated until the dimensions of the previous material were field verified.

CF.   14 16 37 54 80 105 115 130 174

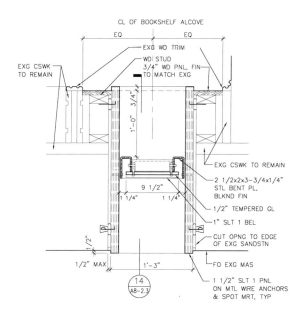

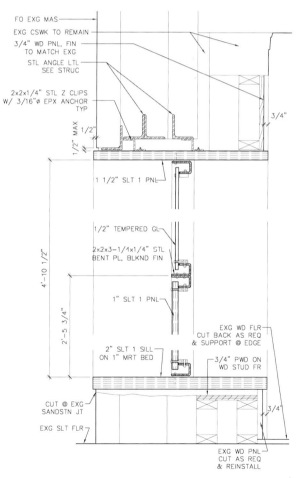

FO EXG MAS

EXG CSWK TO REMAIN

3/4" WD PNL, FIN
TO MATCH EXG

STL ANGLE LTL
SEE STRUC

2x2x1/4" STL Z CLIPS
W/ 3/16"ø EPX ANCHOR
TYP

1/2" MAX

1/2"

3/4"

1 1/2" SLT 1 PNL

1/2" TEMPERED GL

2x2x3-1/1x1/4" STL
BENT PL, BLKND FIN

1" SLT 1 PNL

4'-10 1/2"

2'-5 3/4"

EXG WD FLR
CUT BACK AS REQ
& SUPPORT @ EDGE

2" SLT 1 SILL
ON 1" MRT BED

3/4" PWD ON
WD STUD FR

CUT @ EXG
SANDSTN JT

EXG SLT FLR

3/4"

EXG WD PNL
CUT AS REQ
& REINSTALL

WINDOW SECTION

63

JOINING

Levine We tend to think of joining on the detail level first, but this site comprises multiple buildings, which are taking part in a history of joining. Early on, the client referred to the proposed laboratory as a "bridge building," which would finally complete the circulation of the engineering complex. It is hard to estimate the impact the building will have on the life of its inhabitants, but no longer will departments be isolated at the end of culs-de-sac. The simple act of completing the square discovered an unintended courtyard, which also joins by providing a common point of orientation for those within all the buildings.

CF.   126 176

64

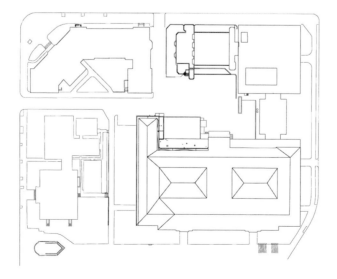

EXISTING SITE PLAN

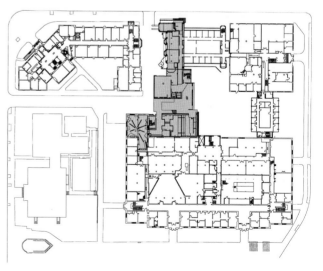

PROPOSED SITE PLAN

LINING

Greenberg

Sykes

Welles

Shapiro

Chestnut Hill

E. Stroudsburg

Berkeley

We think first of a line as just that, a single thread or stroke drawn out or inscribed upon a ground. Though singular in origin, as flax spun into a line of fiber, the line swiftly transforms into a collection of lines so dense that they recede into a plane, and lining is born.

The probable first use of *lining* was for clothing, but the word has an architectural pedigree of nearly equal length. The reasons for lining anything, be it a jacket or a building, arise from necessities of construction, environmental control, patterns of wear, ease of use, and style or appearance. For all these reasons, one layer is often simply not enough. Two or more layers may be necessary to afford stability of construction. Warmth can be enhanced exponentially by multiple layers of materials, and two layers are almost always far more durable than one. Beyond the purely utilitarian, a scrim used as a liner can screen fabrications to alter them to satisfy aesthetic desires. Enhanced purpose is why lining exists.

Like all craft, lining has been exploited in nearly every culture through the perpetual cycle of use, observation, innovation, and production. Lining is used in architecture as structural underlayment, environmental underlayment, scrim or overlayment, and reinforcement.

Structural underlayment is the stable base to which other finishes are attached. It is the core layer of skin that encloses a space, the plane that remains in place as applied layers, both within and without, are altered according to changes in style and means of weather protection. In a multilayered exterior wall, the back-up wall is a type of permanent underlayment. By contrast, form liners in concrete construction are a temporary underlayment that, once removed, leave behind only the memory of their presence imprinted on the surface of the concrete. Just as several

layers of fabric combine, at times, to keep a person warm and dry, so multiple layers of construction at building exteriors combine to provide effective protection against the elements. The principles behind the modern cavity wall and the even more recent rainscreen and pressure-equalized wall give rise to multilayered walls. Finish panels on a back-up wall are a type of liner that, as with a suit jacket, screens the details of construction. While such scrims do not provide literal warmth, they do provide visual and tactile comfort.

A wall—or a building as a wall—at the edge of a field is a type of lining used as visual edging. Just as a cuff forms the edge or boundary of a shirt, the wall lines an edge and delineates a boundary of the field. An arcade along the edge of a building both defines and opens that edge while shielding the inner wall from exposure to weather. A piece of slate or wood at the edge of a window or door both reinforces and emphasizes the opening. Like the collar of a shirt, the slate visually and structurally edges.

The use of the principle of lining gives rise to an architecture of stratification. Unlike much of the architecture of previous centuries, few building elements in the twenty-first century are composed of a single layer of solid material. Discovery and innovation reside in an exponentially expanding array of composite materials. In some cases, the stratification in material generates solid sections, and in other cases, open cavities are deliberately left between layers. Surfaces segregate in accordance with the principles of lining derived from the diversity of purpose. Through forms of lining, we seek actual and aesthetic expression of stratification. Architecture assumes the complexity of geology.

LINING

Greenberg How do you occupy this field? It has little depth without a referent marker: a ship on the sea, a hedgerow, a line of trees. Lines draw attention in the landscape. The house is similar to the lining on the edge of a blanket. The field is the blanket; the house is the boundary lining. It ends and reinforces the blanket of grass, giving the field depth and edge.

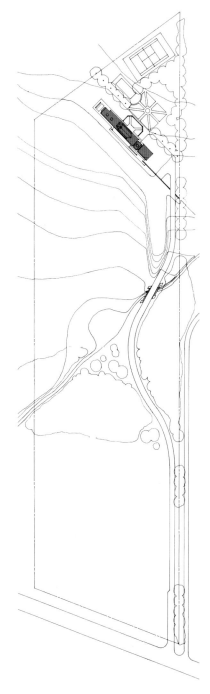

CF. 18 102

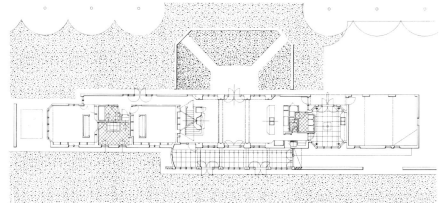

SITE PLAN

FLOOR PLAN

LINING

Sykes The wood panels in this massive assembly hall are similar to the interlining of a coat. They do not add literal warmth, but they provide a perceived warmth against the body. Just as an interlining in clothing design provides a more comfortable feel and less friction with the body, so the wood interlining negotiates the fit of the building exterior on the interior. The panels float free of the concrete, the two elements separated by shadow. A clerestory along the perimeter transmits a further lining of light to the interior.

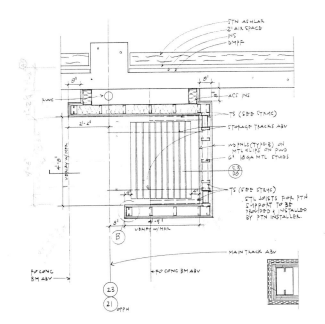

OPERABLE-PANEL PLAN

CF. 37 42 98 104 115 158

70

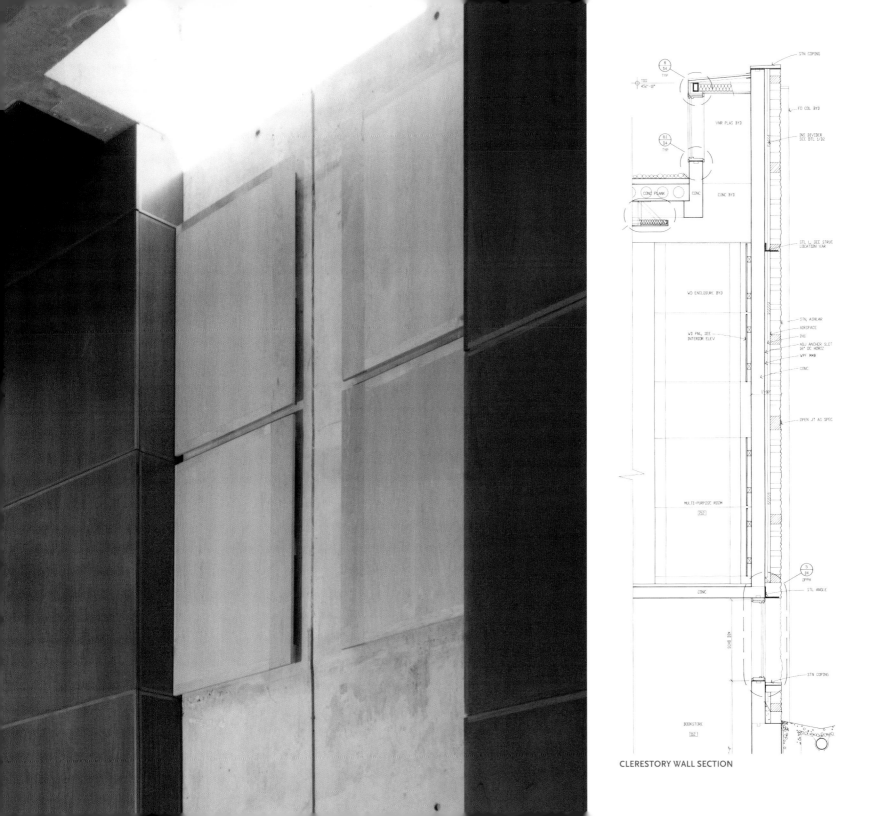

CLERESTORY WALL SECTION

LINING

Welles Initially, we placed the gym floor level with the rest of the school, making the addition too high. The construction manager suggested lowering the floor closer to grade and ramping down from the existing hallway as a more economical solution. The proposed strategy became the source of invention for the entire project. It led to the spatial and material sequencing of brick/block/ramp/brick/block/wood screen/gym. It became the genesis of a double-scale order on the ramp side of the building as a counterpoint to the diminutive order of window boxes opposite.

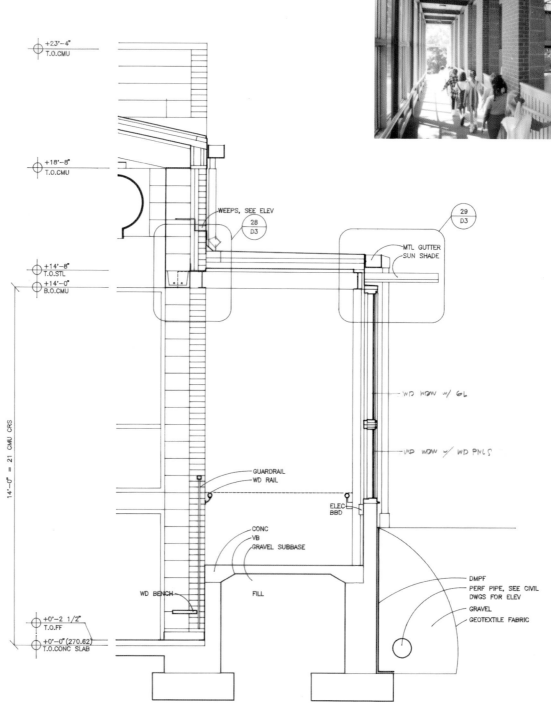

+23'-4"
T.O.CMU

+18'-8"
T.O.CMU

WEEPS, SEE ELEV

28
D3

29
D3

MTL GUTTER
SUN SHADE

+14'-8"
T.O.STL
+14'-0"
B.O.CMU

WD WDW w/ GL

14'-0" = 21 CMU CRS

WD WDW w/ WD PNLS

GUARDRAIL
WD RAIL

ELEC
BBD

CONC
VB
GRAVEL SUBBASE

DMPF
PERF PIPE, SEE CIVIL
DWGS FOR ELEV

WD BENCH

FILL

GRAVEL
GEOTEXTILE FABRIC

+0'-2 1/2"
T.O.FF

+0'-0" (270.62)
T.O.CONC SLAB

CF. 37 112 118 142

RAMP SECTION

LINING

Shapiro Wood paneling is another armoring condition. It provides a durable surface that mirrors the body as it scales the stairs. It also becomes a marker of the hinging condition as the house breaks around the projecting window. The material continuity of the wood lining also highlights and figures the boatlike profile of the stair opening against the hinging of the exterior wall.

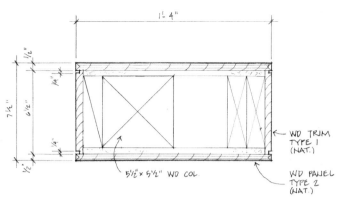

WOOD COLUMN PLAN DETAIL

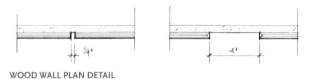

WOOD WALL PLAN DETAIL

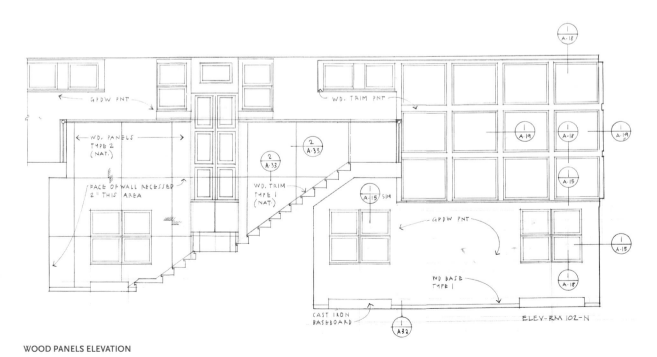

WOOD PANELS ELEVATION

LINING

Chestnut Hill The economics of renovation dictated that the existing terrazzo floor in this student activity room would remain, but a wooden surface was layered over it to accommodate our client's desire for a dance floor. Turning the lining at an incline against the edge wall, the wooden floor became an exaggerated wainscot and spatial boundary as well as a focal point for the large field of the entire room. The same surface turns again to become a table, which is veiled behind the metal screen in the adjacent snack bar.

CF. 60 114 138 164

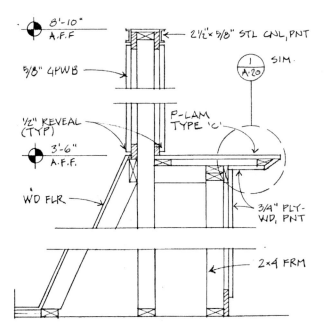

SCREEN WALL SECTION

76

LINING

E. Stroudsburg We originally hoped to use sheets of lead wrapped around plywood substrate for the cladding, but the client was unconvinced. The flamed granite panels are a successful alternative. They project a subtle color shift as one's distance to the building varies.

The modern cavity wall and more recent rainscreen and pressure-equalized principles give rise to multiple layer walls. With open joints to the sides of wall panels—be they slate shingles, brick, or stone—a waterproof liner at the exterior face of the back-up wall provides the interlining that prevents the transmission of water and air through the wall. The exterior material protects the interlining from physical damage, sheds most rain and solar exposure, and provides a visual finish. The requirements that the space between the finish material and the interlining be open to exterior air and generate air pressure equal to the exterior environment give rise to altogether new detail explorations in the expression of this condition.

CF.   44 96 103 156 166

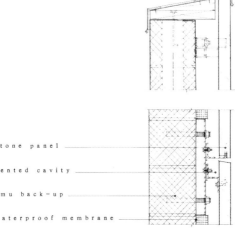

stone panel

vented cavity

cmu back-up

waterproof membrane

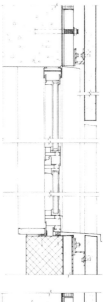

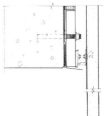

WALL SECTION

LINING

Berkeley The existing leaded-glass windows bore the damage of numerous attempts to keep the cold out. The university had replaced these leaky windows with insulated glass units, but it was nevertheless criticized for not re-creating the subtle effect of true leaded-glass windows, whereby refraction reveals each pane to be handcrafted, slightly out of plane with the others.

Conceptually and technically, the solution became a pressure-equalized window. Venting the chamber between the sealed, integrally gasketed interior glass and the true leaded exterior glass allows the gap between the layer of glass to breathe. Unlike a vacuum-sealed chamber in an insulating glazed unit, this chamber will not fail in fifteen to twenty years. In essence, it was prefailed at the outset, but without the consequence of window damage. Testing revealed the energy efficiency to be nearly equal to a completely sealed, insulating unit.

CF.   14 16 37 54 62 105 115 130 174

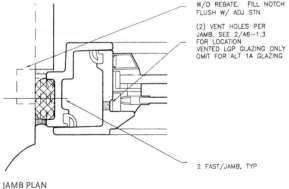

LINE OF STN ⊕ SURROUND W/O REBATE. FILL NOTCH FLUSH W/ ADJ STN

(2) VENT HOLES PER JAMB. SEE 2/A6-1.3 FOR LOCATION VENTED LGP GLAZING ONLY OMIT FOR ALT 1A GLAZING

2 FAST/JAMB, TYP

JAMB PLAN

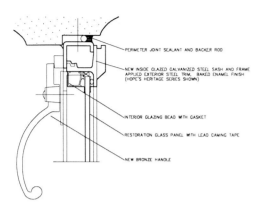

PERIMETER JOINT SEALANT AND BACKER ROD

NEW INSIDE GLAZED GALVANIZED STEEL SASH AND FRAME
APPLIED EXTERIOR STEEL TRIM, BAKED ENAMEL FINISH
(HOPE'S HERITAGE SERIES SHOWN)

INTERIOR GLAZING BEAD WITH GASKET

RESTORATION GLASS PANEL WITH LEAD CAMING TAPE

NEW BRONZE HANDLE

JAMB LATCH

BRONZE HINGE
NOTCH EXTERIOR TRIM AS REQUIRED

JAMB HINGE

REMOVE, REFURBISH AND REGLAZE
EXISTING TRANSOM LPG

24 OZ LCC WEATHER BAR

TRANSOM GLAZING HEAD

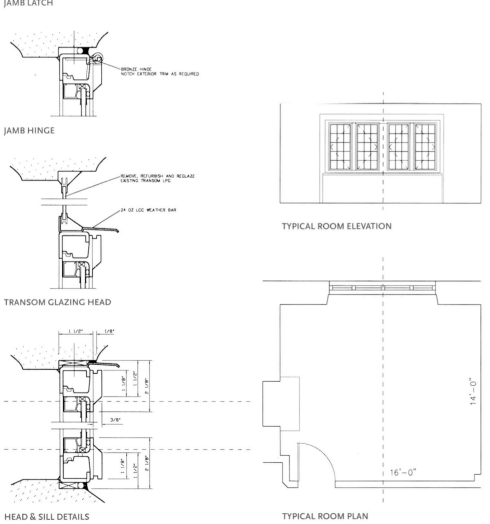

HEAD & SILL DETAILS

TYPICAL ROOM ELEVATION

TYPICAL ROOM PLAN

16'-0"

14'-0"

CALCULATED U VALUE FOR GLAZING OPTIONS

SINGLE GLAZED   1.10
IGU/DOUBLE GLAZED   0.45

COMPARATIVE HEAT LOSS FOR TYPICAL LIVING ROOM

(EQUAL TO TWO TYPICAL BEDROOMS)
OUTSIDE TEMPERATURE   0 °F
INSIDE TEMPERATURE   74°F
AREA OF CONDUCTING SURFACES

	SF	% TOTAL
WINDOW	28	24%
WALL	88	76 %
	116 SF	100 %

SOURCE OF HEAT LOSS	SINGLE GLAZING		IGU/ DOUBLE GLAZING	
	BTU		BTU	
WINDOW CONDUCTION	1870	33%	771	17%
WALL CONDUCTION	1189	21%	1189	26%
INFILTRATION	2669	46%	2669	57%
	5738 BTU	100 %	4630 BTU	100 %

IGU/DOUBLE GLAZING PROVIDES 19% REDUCTION IN TOTAL ROOM HEAT LOSS

LINING

ESP Is the building growing or decaying? What is the difference between growth and decay? We have worked for years to try to stabilize this historic ruin. The elements are winning. This beautiful canvas of life is undergoing an environmental transformation from a programmatic origin to moss. This survey serves as a reminder to us that you do not have to polish everything to achieve beauty. It also reminds us that we can only begin a building; nature, the elements, and changing use and circumstance all ultimately complete and end it. Consideration of the architect's obligation to delay endings is a way to begin.

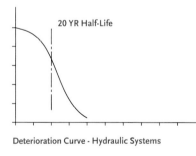

Deterioration Curve - Hydraulic Systems

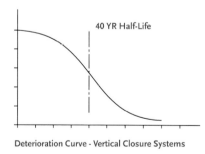

Deterioration Curve - Vertical Closure Systems

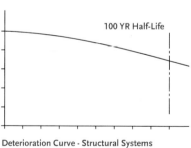

Deterioration Curve - Structural Systems

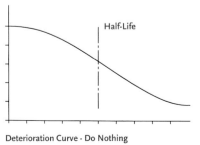

Deterioration Curve - Do Nothing

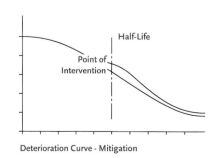

Deterioration Curve - Mitigation

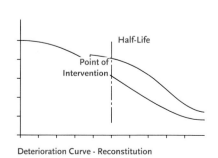

Deterioration Curve - Reconstitution

CF. 36

LINING

Rider S & T Sometimes the architect should stand back and watch processes happen. Here, the evidence of the builder and the sun, while circumstantial, are in the foreground. Some linings are left only as memories. The material forms within the lining. The lining is then stripped—sacrificed to an initially liquid, now solidified core. Fossil-like, the core bears the memory of a long-lost substance—horizontally stratified wood boards. The crudeness of the concrete stair pylon is wonderful. It is itself shadowed from board to board even before the three-dimensional shadows of the struts and mullions begin to trace ever changing patterns across its face in the sun.

Portland Cement Type 1 + Sahara Sand of Falls + Crushed Stone Size #57 + Air Entraining Admixture + Water Reducing Admixture + Accelerating Chloride-Free Admixture + Superplasticizer

CF. 52 102 103

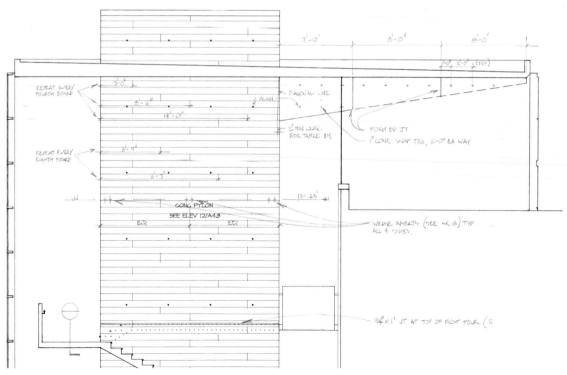

FORMWORK ELEVATION

PATCHING

Sterling

Stafford

Stafford

B & O

E. Stroudsburg

Patching is episodic repair. It fixes only the worn or broken area of an artifact, be it the worn-out elbow of a jacket or the damaged stone of a building stair. It is both expedient and profound, economic and aesthetic.

Like all man-made artifacts, buildings begin to deteriorate from the moment of construction. The rate of deterioration varies from one building component and system to the next, and it is only the rate of degradation, not the process itself, that we can affect. To renew useful life, building stewards have a range of management choices—design choices really—along a continuum from relative continuity to nearly complete discontinuity. They can slow deterioration through the repair of existing materials, restore to a prior condition with new materials, alter to a new form with new materials, passively permit demolition by abandonment and ruin, or actively undertake demolition.

Along this continuum, somewhere between repair and alteration, patching is born. Patching gives a building or its parts new life, but it often does so with deliberately or expediently different material. Although restoration seeks to make an aging artifact new again while returning it to its original appearance, patching has no such objective. Among the impulses that lead most often to the choice of patching in lieu of repair or restoration are economy and expedience. It is a quick fix. Your jacket has a hole in its elbow. You cannot afford a replacement; or you need to continue using the jacket, but no replacement is available. You sew on an elbow patch, and you continue. Familiarity and comfort can also urge patching. You like the jacket. It is not worn; it is well worn. It is broken in, to and around your body. It is an old friend that provides comfort. You do not have to think when you put it on. It is an extension of yourself, so you patch the elbow and continue. Another prompt for patching, albeit a

subtler one, is aesthetic gratification. You enjoy the dialogue between new and old things. The new artifact, the patch, comes into existence against the backdrop of the older one, the jacket. It is not a dialogue of equals; nonetheless, the patch has the potential to tell us a great deal, not only about itself, its time, and circumstance, but also about the original artifact. Patching is typically not a dialogue of union, in that the patch is often joined to the original artifact in a way that permits a return to the pre-patching condition. As such, the patch and the artifact both retain independence, but it is paradoxically a dependent independence, in that the original artifact requires the patch in order to continue being useful, and the patch requires the original artifact in order to have any meaningful existence.

During the past century, the reputation of patching, rarely exalted, has fallen on particularly hard times in most economically advanced cultures. Patching is generally relegated to the status of a necessary expedience, occasionally required but rarely desirable. Contemporary culture usually prefers replacement or even abandonment. Patching is seen as a temporary, stopgap measure on the way to a comprehensive "lasting" solution, such as a new jacket or a new house. It gives renewed life with a minimum of material and energy. It is an act of design most often undertaken by those who do not think of themselves as designers, yet it is the ultimate form of ecological responsibility.

Sykes

PATCHING

Sterling Formerly a window, this stone opening now acts as a portal between different areas of the expanded servery. The plinth block at the bottom patches the stone cut underneath the window and is profiled to ease people through the new opening. Concealing the scar on the stone jambs left by the old window frame is a shadow cast by new stainless-steel channels. We did not know whether the limestone was bearing the wall, so we had the channels provide additional support at the opening head, where the removal of an intermediate stone window jamb brought structural questions into play. The circumstance of masking the hole also serves to protect the stone from equipment as it passes between the two spaces.

Our drawings showed the big limestone plinth blocks set in two pieces. A deal was struck with the masons: "Give us those plinths in one piece, and we'll let you cut false joints in that archway over the back door." They each weigh more than 1200 pounds.

CF.   38 105 122 154 180

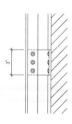

SECTION DETAIL

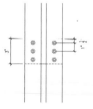

ELEVATION DETAIL

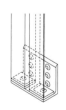

ISOMETRIC DETAIL

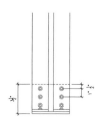

BASE ELEVATION

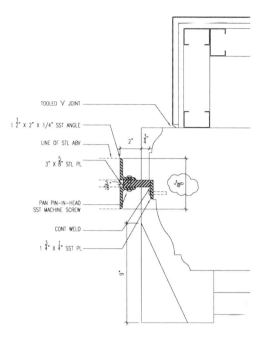

UPPER SST JAMB PLAN

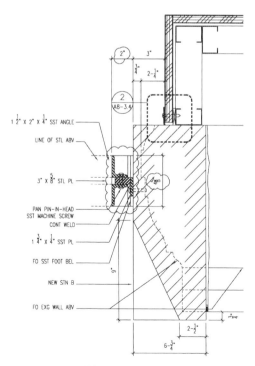

LOWER SST JAMB PLAN

89

PATCHING

Stafford When we first entered this part of the building, it felt like we were on an archaeological tour of Rome. If it had been dripping and moss covered, it would be the Domus Aurea. Previously an uninhabited basement, the stone and brick arches were the foundation for the rest of the residence hall and created such a compelling space that we were reluctant to tear them out to fit in the new program. Instead, we made minor cuts where necessary and distinguished our action from the existing stonework with slate panels.

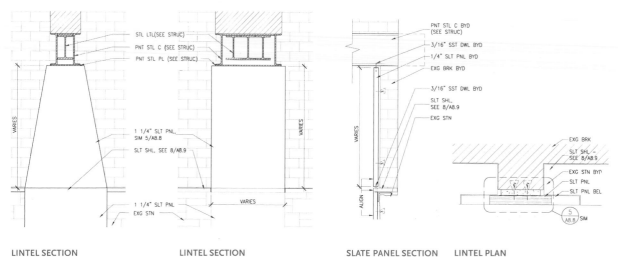

LINTEL SECTION   LINTEL SECTION   SLATE PANEL SECTION   LINTEL PLAN

PATCHING

Stafford To give privacy to the student rooms without destroying the archway structure, we bricked them in. We were trying to decide between more than fifteen different brick patterns at a pin-up when, in a moment, someone remarked: "Why choose? Use them all!" If you're going to make a patch, it should be a really interesting one. The mason said it was the best job he had ever worked on and even brought his grandchildren to the site to show off his handiwork. Unusual as it is for a contractor to show such pride in his craft, it is even more uncommon to receive from the parent of a student an unsolicited letter comparing our work here to his tour of European castles.

CF.   90 105

92

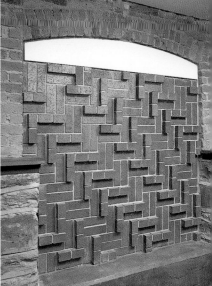

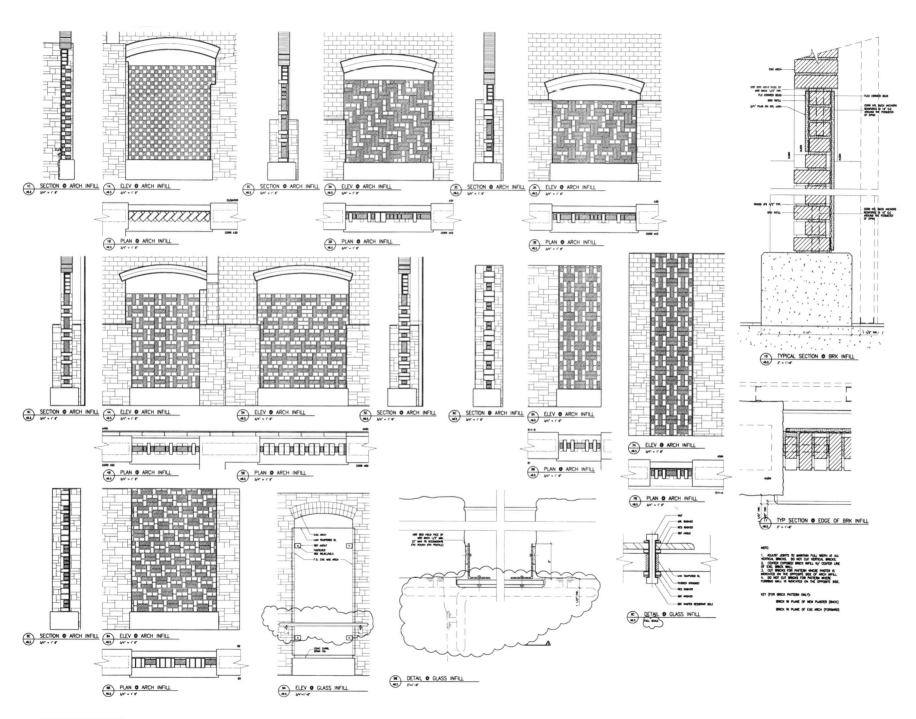

PATCHING

B & O The hundred-foot-long clear-span structure was failing, but to avoid ripping the roof off this wonderful railroad-car shop—now a museum—we devised a post-tensioned "sister" to each truss. With a clerk-in-the-works type project such as this, one finds love in whatever details need fixing. In this case, a simple bracket for additional wood members and the bottom steel chord solved the problem that needed solving within the museum's modest means.

According to modern engineering research, which considers wood's species and grade, the magnitude and duration of loading, and other factors, the trusses had been overstressed for some years (likely since their original installation). This resulted in a systemic shear failure at the heel joints of nearly every truss. Additionally, years of unattended water infiltration had further weakened the timber structure.

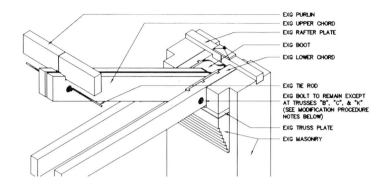

EXISTING TRUSS CONFIGURATION

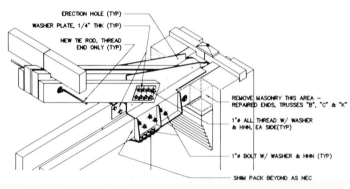

NEW TRUSS CONFIGURATION

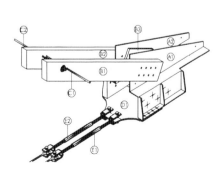

NEW COMPONENTS

PATCHING

E. Stroudsburg Two spatial patches bracket the north and south ends of the existing brick building. These patches repaired the relationship of a prior building to the site. One patch reestablishes the building-to-street relationship, while the other reconnects the separated residential and academic campuses. Internally, light is the primary mediator, drawing attention to the boundary between the old and new portions of the building and illuminating the now landlocked classrooms of the existing structure. The formerly exterior wall is exposed on the interior, along with the original window and door frames, as a remnant of the old enclosure.

CF. 44 78 103 156 166

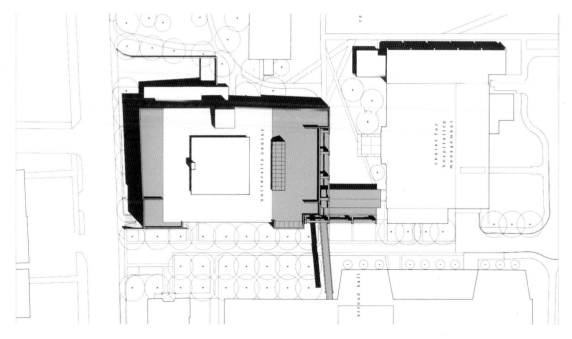

SITE PLAN

PATCHING

Sykes Rotated forty-five degrees from the street and clad only in brick, the original student union had little to do with anything except itself. An abstraction of collegiate gothic, which resulted in a sort of hacked-away cathedral, the student union now provides a contrast to and an inversion of the fairly monolithic nearby buildings. This articulation of the concrete frame lets the casual passerby perceive the wall as permeable and is an effective means of drawing attention to the more important public spaces.

CF. 37 42 70 104 115 158

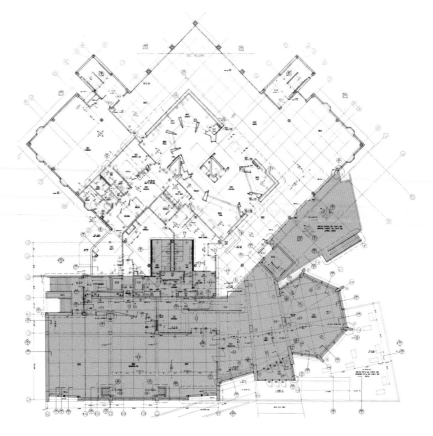

FIRST LEVEL PLAN

PROFILING

Berkeley

Rider A & F

Shipley

Villanova

Welles

Profiling occurs at edges or boundaries, where physical form ceases. In architecture, as in life, edges and boundaries offer an abstract of the wider understanding to come and are the moments most fraught with danger as well as opportunity for invention. Our first visual impressions are generally of mass. It is the silhouette—the profile revealing the boundary between what is and is not—that enters next into consciousness. The black sheet of paper cut to reveal the flattened boundary of the human head against a white ground, the shape of a mountain or cliff seen at great distance or at dusk or in moonlight, the outline of a building just coming into view on the horizon—these are among the first signals we receive of the approaching world, be it human, natural, or constructed. In this strictly perceptual sense, first encounters are of a strongly backlit world, which provides little detail beyond a profile and renders substance as shadow.

Profiling gives us the first clue to beginnings and endings, size and shape, direction and focus. In the constructed world, as in all large formations of the earth's topography, profiling exists at the margins of earth and sky. The first architectural profiles occur at the boundaries where building ceases and the natural or urban worlds begin. Boundaries and edges are signals in the natural and constructed worlds. The edge itself—the precise shape and location of the profile—waxes and wanes with time and circumstance, but the substance evolves more quickly. Profiling, the boundary between one thing and another—between forest and sky, ground and building, or building and sky—defines these edges of our first perception and provides our first understanding.

As in nature, boundaries between building elements generally occur where planes meet, change direction, or end. The sources of invention in profiling are diverse, but construction technology and stylistic preference are the main inspiration. Architectural profiling has been richest historically in permutations at the union of wall and roof, where building meets sky on the outside and wall meets ceiling on the inside. The joining of roof and wall is also one of the most frequent moments of technological failure in buildings. One system, the wall, ends where another, the roof, begins and where exposure to the natural elements of rain, snow, ice, and wind is greatest. Profiles of all sorts have been invented to close and conceal this junction of wall and roof. All languages of architecture have developed both generic and specific profiling idioms to close and signal eave, base, and guardrail. Profiling both forms and shapes these joints and terminations. When a roof overhangs a wall, for example, the principal line of profiling is at the outermost edge of the roof overhang; but when the roof remains behind the wall, profiling creates the technical closure and the visual binding.

It is the challenge and the promise of profiling to find itself placed between two realms: wall and ground, roof and sky, platform and opening. Always between, never center stage, profiling edges bottoms, tops, and sides. Owing perhaps to its literal position at the periphery of architecture, it is often overlooked, unattended. Yet it is through profiling—by limiting, defining, and developing at the boundaries—that we come to explore and know surface and space.

PROFILING

Nowhere else in a building does the body come into such intimate contact with public regulation as it does on a stair. This range of guards shows the adjustment and accounting for a detail that is elemental to architecture. Codes change, as does one's approach. For instance, if one looks at many guardrails today, the vertical picket spacing is determined solely by the code. This proportion has become mundane to the extreme—a situation we have reacted to as a creative impetus. This is our way of asserting responsibility for the architecture: a code official did not design this; we did. We view the code as another constraint, to make the architecture richer. The codes have become a driver to creativity that never existed before. Now there is something to interpret, to respond to. Railings begin with legal or social intentions; one then composes law into art.

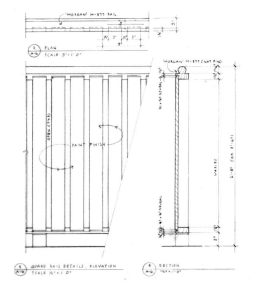
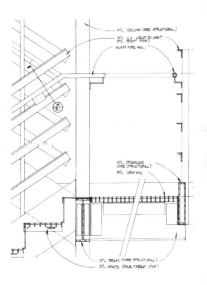

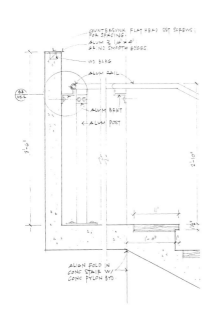

COUNTERSUNK FLAT HEAD SST SCREWS FOR SPACING
ALUM R 1/8 x 4" GRIND SMOOTH EDGES
WD BLKG
ALUM RAIL
ALUM BRKT
ALUM POST
ALIGN FOLD IN CONC STAIR W/ CONC PYLON BYD

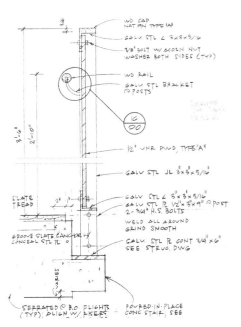

WD CAP NAT FIN TYPE IN
GALV STL L 3x8x5/16
3/8" BOLT W/ACORN NUT WASHER BOTH SIDES (TYP)
WD RAIL
GALV STL BRACKET @ POSTS
1/2" UNR PWD, TYPE "A"
GALV STL JL 3x3x5/16
SLATE TREAD
GALV STL L 3"x3"x5/16"
GALV STL R 1/2"x 2"x 9" @ POST 2-3/4" H.S. BOLTS
WELD ALL AROUND GRIND SMOOTH
GALV STL R CONT 3/4"x6" SEE STRUC. DWG
GROOVE SLATE @ANCHOR W/ CONCEAL STL R
SERRATED @ B.O. FLIGHTS (TYP); ALIGN W/ RISERS
POURED-IN-PLACE CONC STAIR, SEE

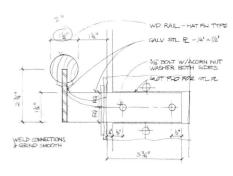

2"
1 1/2"
WD RAIL - NAT FIN TYPE
GALV STL R - 1/4"x 1 1/2"
3/8" BOLT W/ACORN NUT WASHER BOTH SIDES
SLOT R.D FOR STL R
WELD CONNECTIONS & GRIND SMOOTH
3 3/4"

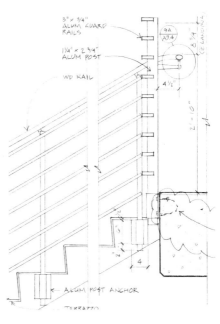

3"x 3/4" ALUM GUARD RAILS
1 1/4"x 2 3/4" ALUM POST
WD RAIL
ALUM POST ANCHOR
TERRAZZO

PROFILING

Holes in building floors or at the edges of elevated platforms are common boundaries for accommodating stairs and ramps. Like roof edge and wall base, such openings are moments of danger, albeit more human and less technological in origin. The guard contains the body to the stair or landing, and prevents it from falling. The handrail, literally formed to the hand, supports the body as it scales the building. The continuity of body movement as it rises and descends translates into the continuity of the handrail.

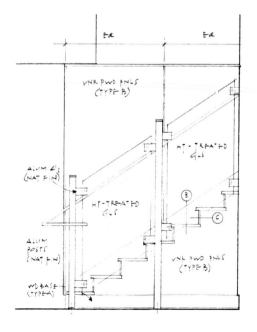
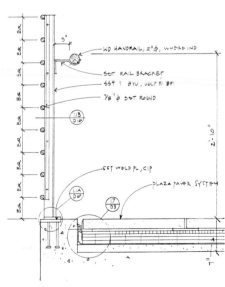
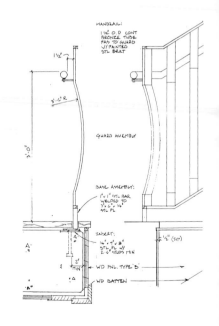

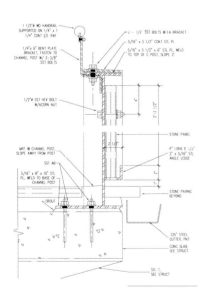

1 1/2"∅ WD HANDRAIL
SUPPORTED ON 1/4" x 1
1/4" CONT STL RAIL

1/4"x 6" BENT PLATE
BRACKET, FASTEN TO
CHANNEL POST W/ 2-3/8"
SST BOLTS

1/2"∅ SST HEX BOLT
W/ACORN NUT

2 - 1/2" SST BOLTS @ EA BRACKET

5/16" x 5 1/2" CONT STL RAIL

5/16" x 5 1/2" x 6" STL PL, WELD
TO TOP OF C POST, SLOPE 2"

STONE PANEL

MRT @ CHANNEL POST,
SLOPE AWAY FROM POST

SST AB

5/16" x 8" x 10" STL
PL, WELD TO BASE OF
CHANNEL POST

GROUT

6" LONG L 1 1/2"
2" x 5/16" STL
ANGLE LEDGE

STONE PAVING
BEYOND

.125" STEEL
GUTTER, PNT

CONC SLAB,
SEE STRUCT

STL T,
SEE STRUCT

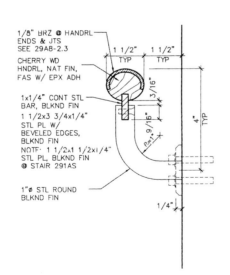

1/8" BRZ @ HANDRL
ENDS & JTS
SEE 29A8-2.3

CHERRY WD
HNDRL, NAT FIN,
FAS W/ EPX ADH

1x1/4" CONT STL
BAR, BLKND FIN
1 1/2x3 3/4x1/4"
STL PL W/
BEVELED EDGES,
BLKND FIN
NOTE: 1 1/2x1 1/2x1/4"
STL PL, BLKND FIN
@ STAIR 291AS

1"∅ STL ROUND
BLKND FIN

1 1/2"
TYP

1 1/2"
TYP

3/16"

4"
TYP

1/4"

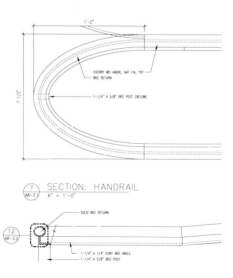

1'-2"

7 1/2"

CHERRY WD HNDRL, NAT FIN, TYP
BRZ RETURN

1-1/4" x 5/8" BRZ POST (BELOW)

⑦ SECTION: HANDRAIL
A8-3.1   6" = 1'-0"

⑫
A8-3.2

SOLID BRZ RETURN

1-1/4" x 1/4" CONT BRZ ANGLE
1-1/4" x 5/8" BRZ POST

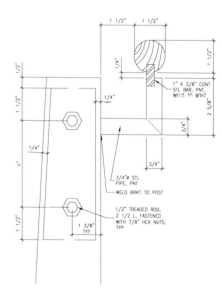

1 1/2"   1 1/2"

1/4"

1 1/2"

1/2"

1/4"

4"

1 1/2"

1 3/8"
TYP

3/4"

3/4"

2 5/8"

1" X 3/8" CONT
STL BAR, PNT,
WELD TO BRKT

3/4"∅ STL
PIPE, PNT
WELD BRKT TO POST

1/2" TREADED ROD,
2 1/2 L, FASTENED
WITH 7/8" HEX NUTS,
TYP

PROFILING

Rider A & F The junction between roof and wall is so often a chunky disappointment in this inexpensive construction type (a four- to six-inch flap of light gauge, often oilcanned, metal). We worked to use shadow as the detail instead of broad, flat metal overlapping the wall. The copings typically extend a few inches beyond the face of the wall, with minimal overlaps of the surface of the wall.

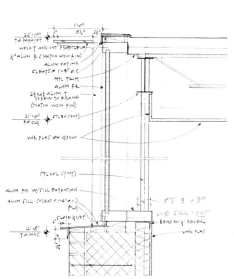

WINDOW HEAD SECTION

The aluminum coping had to be of sufficient gauge to maintain rigidity and planarity. For unsupported projecting pieces, the thickness was as great as a half inch to prevent oilcanning. For the standard coping condition we specified .090 inches.

CF.   104 144 148

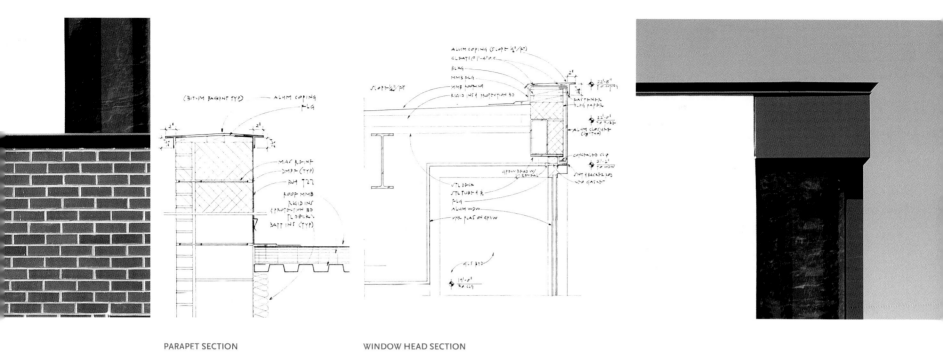

PARAPET SECTION   WINDOW HEAD SECTION

PROFILING

Shipley This building is an essay in profiling, in outlining. It is fully bounded by lead-coated copper outlines. Slate panels are finished and contained by light-gauge channels, which outline the boundaries between materials. Brick-and block-bearing walls have lead-coated copper caps. The shadow at these caps is exaggerated by the projection of the cap flashing beyond the wall. Metal visors finish each slate panel at the top, drawing the eye to the broad shadow cast below. Parapet sheathing is set back in plane with the wall, well behind the visor. The profiling here is not smooth and continuous. It is crude and purposefully disrupted panel by panel.

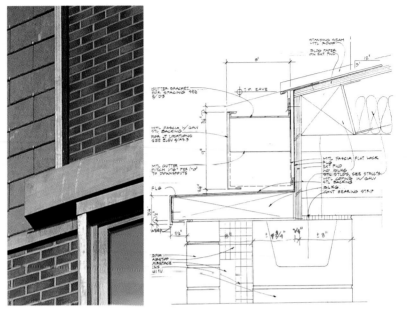

GUTTER SECTION   EAVE SECTION

CF.   24 30 36 56 103 114 115 120 132 136 150 168

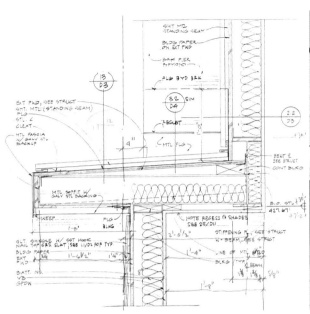

BROW SECTION

PROFILING

Villanova   The university advertised this project with an answer: a bridge. We replied with a definition of the problem (the movement of students across the road) and a series of possible solutions, one of which was to build nothing. If the best answer were to hire a traffic engineer to analyze traffic signals, then we would be happy to do that and leave. A bridge for pedestrians would have required an impractical quarter-mile ramp for accessibility. Instead, a cut in the earth—a negative profile— was carved to bridge cars over people. The profile was widened and lined with gingko trees, a lawn, and a dolomitic-limestone retaining wall, expressing the strategy as a path in the landscape rather than as a tunnel. The ground is thus profiled in reverse, carved away rather than added to.

Given the 7,000 students using the crosswalk on a daily basis, the university sought to unite the parking lot with the main campus as a major campus gateway.

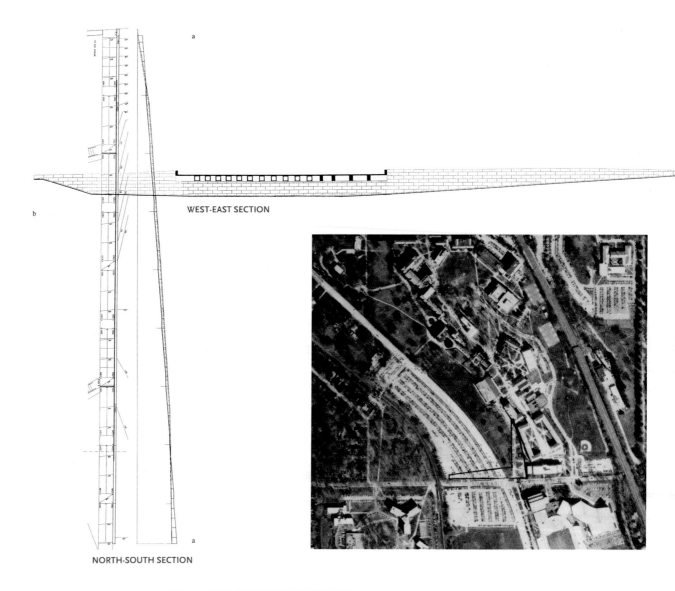

WEST-EAST SECTION

NORTH-SOUTH SECTION

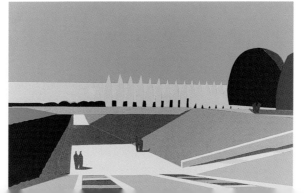

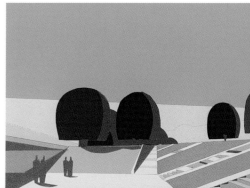

PROFILING

Welles The union between gym and ground, between landform and surface, is another act of profiling. This moment of planar change is again a locus of much elemental danger, from active-water penetration to rising damp to insect infestation to human wear. A concrete base negotiates the natural ground–to–building relationship on one side while a stoop-lined playground provides an urban profile on the side opposite. In classical terms, the thickened wall, water table, or column pedestal all represent base profiling—born in construction, then shaped and formed in the mind and eye of convention—which defines the separation of wall from ground. In contemporary terms, base profiling both separates and unifies wall and ground. It underlines and draws attention to distinctions, or it conceals distinctions, depending on intention.

CF. 37 72 118 142

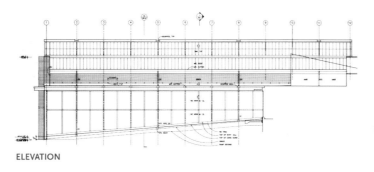

ELEVATION

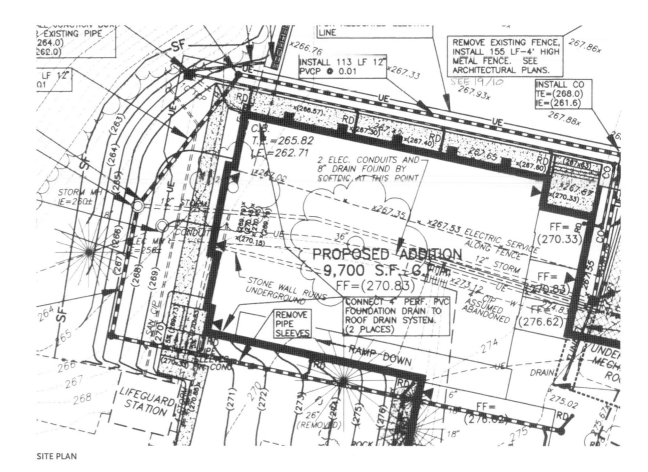

SITE PLAN

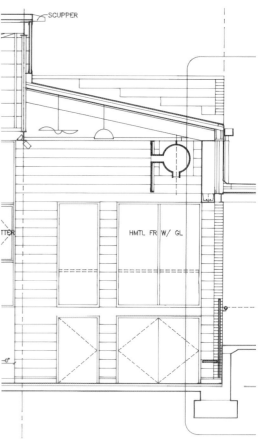

SCUPPER

HMTL FR W/ GL

BUILDING SECTION

PROFILING

Places to sit abound in our work. We seek them out as permanent, not just movable elements. We seek out the seat in surprising places. Where they end, we sometimes experience their section as profile, as elevation. This is abrupt profiling, very elemental and powerful. It is a slab, not a place to linger long or in comfort, but appropriate for an entry or a lobby. At the opposite end of the bench-profiling spectrum are banquette seats, edged by two-dimensional profiles that mirror the shape of the seated body. These profiles contain the body. They are both physical and psychological, preventing one from sliding off the end of the bench as they bound seats and tables, transforming them from furniture to architecture.

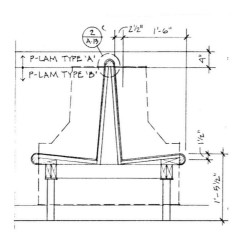

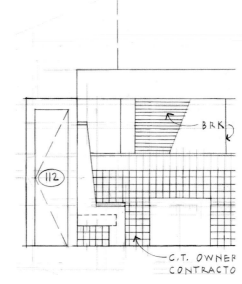

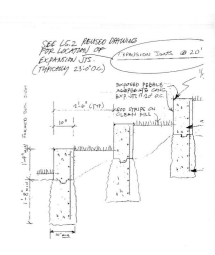

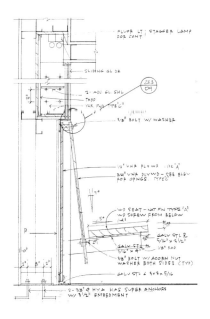
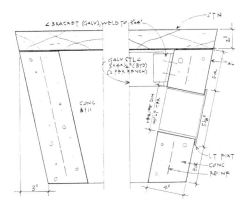
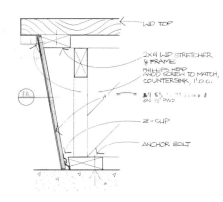
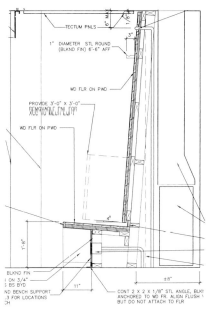

SCALING

Welles

Shipley

Sterling

Scott

Levine

Chiller

Scaling has several significant uses in architecture. One is to extrapolate the full understanding of a completed form from its less than full–scale representation. Another is to correlate the size of architectural elements with the size of the human body. Still another is to regulate into a unified whole the steps or stages of construction elements and the intervals between them, much as the scaling ladder is ordered in regularly repeated rungs.

Nearly all architecture begins with drawings, models, and other efforts to conceptualize and develop a proposed world before constructing it. Scaling allows us to represent and manipulate a slice of the larger world at less than actual size. Without representational scaling, science and architecture might grind to a halt. The rules of proportion allow us to rely on a given correlation between representation and reality and to communicate that relation to others. In architecture, scaling is the means of communication that allows users of buildings to understand how well a proposal answers their needs and desires. Scaling is also the way conceivers communicate their intention to constructors.

Another use of the word *scaling* relates the standard size of elements of architecture to the human body. Most building parts, whether a doorknob or lever, a handrail on a stair, a stair riser or tread, have a relatively small range of conventional sizes. Manufacturers of building products and architects alike generally accept this small range as a given, and building safety standards in many societies have defined maximum and minimum sizes of various architectural elements in their building codes. These sizes, both conventional and legally required, have been empirically derived by reference to the human body. Our intuitive understanding of size continues to derive from reference to the human body. When we say an object or space has intimate scale, we mean that the size closely approximates that of the body. When we say it has large scale, we mean that the size dwarfs the

body. When we say that an object has no scale, we mean that we cannot comprehend how large it is, that the object provides insufficient clues to its size, large or small. Since correlations between body size and architecture have evolved to become scaling conventions, deviations from the conventions have special significance. Scaling is not only the controlling mechanism by which we strive to fit the human body, but it is also the ordering system that allows architecture to misfit the human body purposefully.

Scaling also provides the visual and construction means to organize building elements into coherent patterns and assemblages. In the modern musical scale, tuning is the frequency ratio from note to note, where notes are organized by their frequencies into a series of eight tones, called an octave. In architecture, repetitive functional and visual elements, such as the mullions of interior and exterior glass walls, can be similarly organized by scaling. Scaling of glass size can be repetitive, with each piece the same size or additive, with larger panels assembled from many smaller ones, "note" by "note," as numerical scaling guides the differential sizes and relations among the elements. Such a wall may be said to possess scale, meaning that small units progress into larger units, providing cues to the range of absolute and relative size.

Scaling is the mathematical system that brings rule and measure to visual perception. It is a discipline in which the human body is the unit of measure that houses the hidden soul of architecture.

Berkeley

Shipley

SCALING

Welles A good test of a building is using it for an unintended purpose. For the Welles Activity Center, this test came shortly after the gym's opening. A church service was held in the basilica-like gym. In his sermon, the minister described his discovery of the building's intentions. Initially, he had wondered about all the miniature window boxes, but since the service got under way, he saw that they were crowded with the congregation's children. For us, the window boxes arose as a device to mediate between the large space needed for basketball and a space scaled to the bodies and minds of lower school children. An adult can't enter this children's space unless willing to contort his or her body to the child's shape. While the windows started inside, they eventually pushed their way outside. There the window boxes form the edge of a blacktop playground with a reference to row house stoops and the urban streetscape.

CF. 37 72 112 142

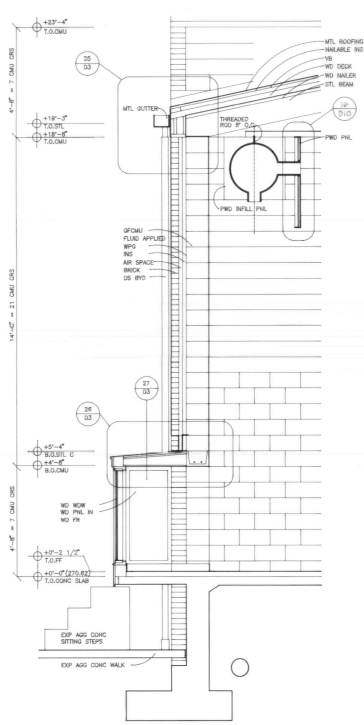

WALL SECTION

SCALING

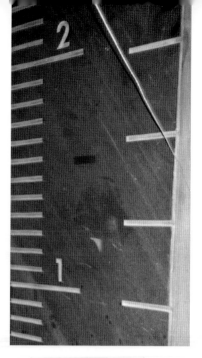

Shipley Children take every available opportunity to measure themselves, especially during the middle school years, the age of greatest change. In this building, the section grows with the children as they move up the grades. It is lowest for the sixth graders on the first floor. It is highest for the eighth graders on the third floor. The slate column covers overtly manifest the three "r's": reading, 'riting, and 'rithmetic. At the same time, they acknowledge scaling. An eye chart uses letters to reference visual scaling and the role of distance in the perception of size. It is about relative scaling. On another floor, a measuring stick designed in the slate column cover reveals actual size. It is not only fun for the children to measure themselves, but it is also a lesson in absolute scaling. The levels and layers in the details become metaphors for the constructive and programmatic facts of the school.

CF. 24 30 36 56 103 108 114 115 132 136
150 168

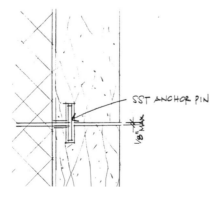

COLUMN SECTION

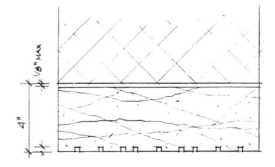

COLUMN PLAN

SCALING

Sterling   In this project, we were working adjacent to a craft tradition, where all parties involved in the construction understood scaling implicitly. While code provides a range of answers regarding toe clearances and the like, it is that dimension in the context of everything else that needs to be tuned: what is the circumference of the foot relative to the counter leg, relative to the wall? Additionally, scaling is an issue of tactility: what does the hand touch as it slides the tray along the food line?

The schedule required the casework to be built off-site long before the stainless-steel wall panels could be hung and field verified. This little space is deceiving in its simplicity but extraordinary in its constructional complexity; the casework pieces had to fit precisely into recesses carved out of the fractured exterior wall. The Canadian fabricators had never worked with an architect who came to the plant asking to see connection hardware.

CF. 38 88 105 154 180

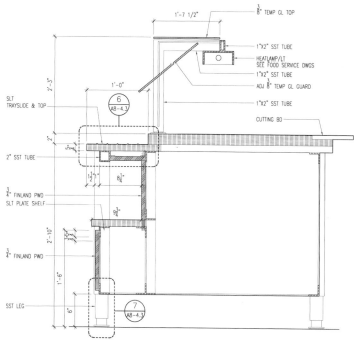

SERVERY COUNTER SECTION

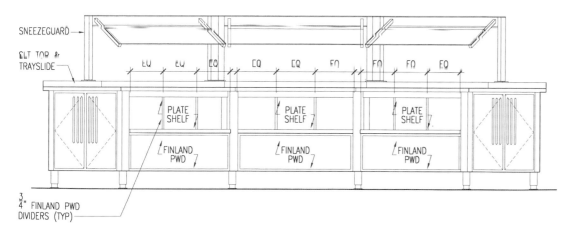

SNEEZEGUARD

SLT TOP &
TRAYSLIDE

EQ EQ EQ   EQ   EQ   EQ   EQ   EQ   EQ

PLATE
SHELF

PLATE
SHELF

PLATE
SHELF

FINLAND
PWD

FINLAND
PWD

FINLAND
PWD

3/4" FINLAND PWD
DIVIDERS (TYP)

SERVERY-COUNTER ELEVATION

SCALING

Scott This wall was conceived as a type of tapestry or mural for the display of everyday bathing artifacts and activities. Fragmentation of a very long space is achieved by varying the opacity of the glass. At the shower, the glass is clear. At the exterior windows, it is obscure. Along the wall, it is either mirrored or back painted. The glass units are of regular, repetitive size, but the patterns of back painted white, black, and grey vary from piece to piece.

The glass panels are adhered to the substrate with mastic, and a gap between adjacent panels prevents moisture from getting trapped behind the glass wall. Because of the direct-adhered application and our concerns about the long-term effect of humidity, the adhesion of the paint to the glass was critical. We found that most architectural paints, such as latex, enamel, and epoxies, have poor long-term adhesion when applied directly to glass. Working with a local glass artist, we had success with a baked-on powder-coat finish usually used on metal similar to a Tiger Drylac product.

CF. 20

MIRROR WALL COLLAGE

SCALING

Levine   The question for us was how to domesticate glass in the surrounding context of brick. Before the careful modulation from small to large elements, the client is able to relate the common language of proportion, inherent in the existing construction, to this modern cladding system. Rather than designing enormous, uninterrupted panes of glass, we related the curtainwall dimensions to the fenestration of the neighboring buildings. This contextual joining comforted the client about the installation of a modern curtain wall within an older fabric.

The inner and outer glass units form an air plenum, through which room-return air is circulated and extracted via the HVAC system. The intermediate blind reflects some of the solar radiation incident on the facade back through the external glass unit and absorbs the remaining radiation, re-radiating it back into the cavity as heat. The heat is then extracted via the continuous airflow between the inner and outer glass units.

CF. 64 176

126

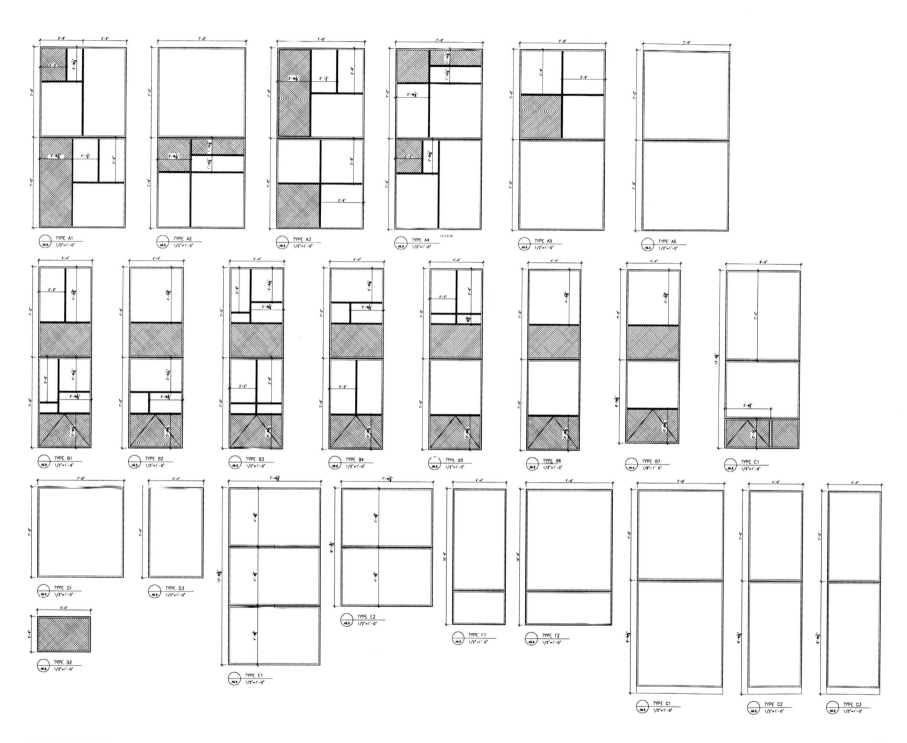

WINDOW SCHEDULE

SCALING

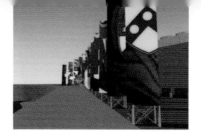

Chiller From the highways that weave and intertwine around the site, the pylons are experienced as alternating rhythms of information and landscape. Seen obliquely as one exits the eastbound expressway toward the university, the pylons close and form a momentarily complete graphic image. When seen from the south side of the rail underpass as one leaves the university, they again close momentarily to form an ivy-covered scrim. From other positions as one approaches or moves through the site, they are seen both as independent, fragmentary objects and as a larger, complete, landscaped gateway, encompassing the perimeter of the site. The changing point of view generates both a large-scale wall and a relatively open, smaller-scale collection of individual pylons.

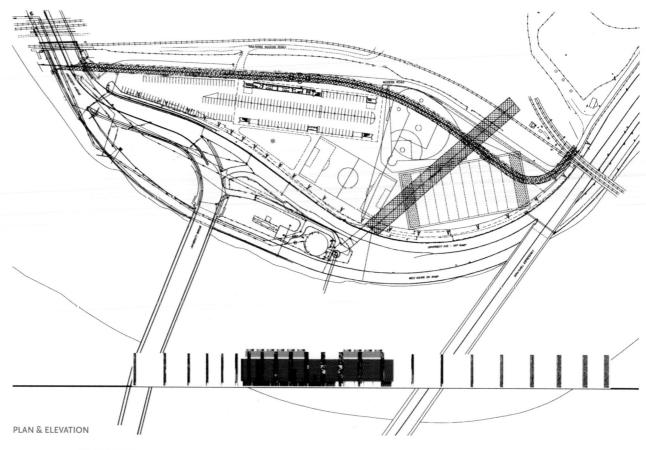

PLAN & ELEVATION

SCALING

Berkeley Detail is not about replicating or even interpreting a style. It is about scale. Do not confuse styling for scaling by letting a selecting circumstance determine a scaling circumstance. For instance, we could have left the guard design at the required four-inch vertical space, but an interest in the rhythm of climbing turned a code requirement into an opportunity for dimensional refinement and syncopation. Doubling the post led to concerns about the size of the hex nut and its relationship to the steel lip, which in turn led to the consideration of installation and fabrication clearances. The result is a stepped scale composed of double rails, attachment plates, and hex-nut fasteners.

CF. 14 16 37 54 62 80 105 115 174

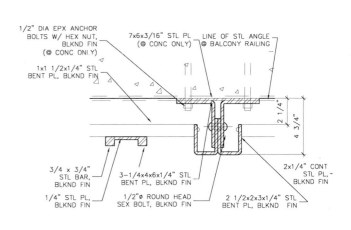

1/2" DIA EPX ANCHOR BOLTS W/ HEX NUT, BLKND FIN (@ CONC ONLY)

7x6x3/16" STL PL (@ CONC ONLY)

LINE OF STL ANGLE @ BALCONY RAILING

1x1 1/2x1/4" STL BENT PL, BLKND FIN

2 1/4"

4 3/4"

3/4 x 3/4" STL BAR, BLKND FIN

1/4" STL PL, BLKND FIN

3-1/4x4x6x1/4" STL BENT PL, BLKND FIN

1/2"ø ROUND HEAD SEX BOLT, BLKND FIN

2x1/4" CONT STL PL, BLKND FIN

2 1/2x2x3x1/4" STL BENT PL, BLKND FIN

STAIR GUARD PLAN

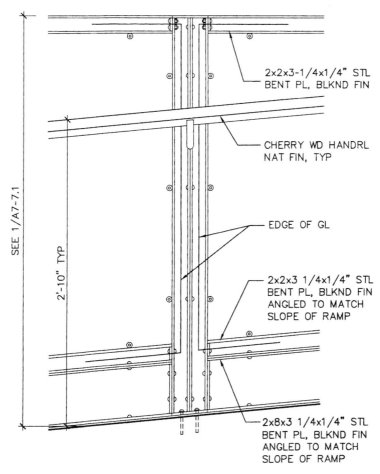

SEE 1/A7-7.1

2'-10" TYP

2x2x3-1/4x1/4" STL
BENT PL, BLKND FIN

CHERRY WD HANDRL
NAT FIN, TYP

EDGE OF GL

2x2x3 1/4x1/4" STL
BENT PL, BLKND FIN
ANGLED TO MATCH
SLOPE OF RAMP

2x8x3 1/4x1/4" STL
BENT PL, BLKND FIN
ANGLED TO MATCH
SLOPE OF RAMP

RAMP ELEVATION

131

SCALING

Shipley You cannot climb the ceiling, but that is precisely why you remember this stair. The contractor did a superb job building the sharp edges in concrete; however, there was some staining due to improper preparation of the stair form. In retrospect, it is a mark of construction; but at the time, not anticipating this sort of imperfection was irritating. A further reminder of the vertical scale of the school is the brick soap inserted into the concrete-block wall. Accommodating the floor plank, the brick makes up the full concrete-block course and marks the floor.

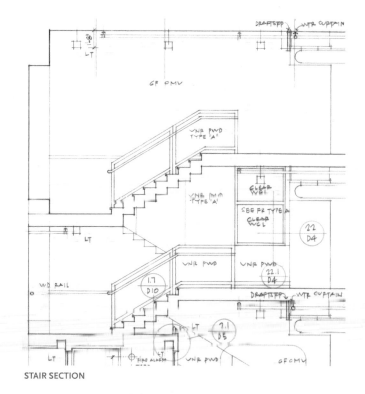

STAIR SECTION

CF.   24 30 36 56 103 108 114 115 120 136
      150 168

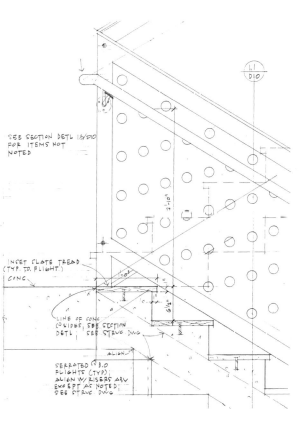

SEE SECTION DETL 13/D10
FOR ITEMS NOT
NOTED

INSET SLATE TREAD
(TYP. TO FLIGHT)

CONC

LINE OF CONC
(3 SIDES, SEE SECTION
DETL) SEE STRUC DWG

ALIGN

SERRATED ∼3.0
FLIGHTS (TYP);
ALIGN W/ RISERS ABV
EXCEPT AS NOTED;
SEE STRUC DWG

STAIR SECTION DETAIL   133

SELECTING

Shipley

Chestnut Hill

Kegler

Welles

The number of selections we make, accepted as design or not, is staggering. Making these thousands of selections occupies a significant portion of the energy that goes into our buildings. The selecting we speak of here is not the ancient act of choosing raw materials and basic building systems. Rather, what we refer to is the vast array of already designed and manufactured products and systems that form the web of choice in which all who build in advanced economies operate—sometimes happily but unknowingly, occasionally knowingly but unhappily, and only rarely knowingly, provocatively, and happily.

Today, hundreds of thousands of building products are on view in every architect's office, electronically as well as physically in back-of-house catalogs. These products permeate all aspects of life in the developed world. At the same time, these already designed and manufactured products are the stuff that give the reflective and aspiring architect the greatest unease. What is it about the Sweet's Catalog and other seemingly endless sources of product information that generates such massive denial? What are the theoretical and actual losses that we accrue through this denial? Why have we so few present-day theories of selection?

The anxiety surrounding selecting, which we first began to feel during the industrial revolution, lies in the difference between suggestion and actualization, between manipulation and inclusion. It is an anxiety borne of the ambivalence we continue to experience regarding a culture formerly of textual selection carried out by custom production, but which is currently the opposite: a culture of custom texts supported by mass production. In earlier times, we agreed to texts as the means to begin selecting and accepted the creative domain as the organization of selections into custom assemblages. Today, we create custom texts and are rendered anxious by the myth of a custom production that is based in large measure on mass-replicated building products.

Architectural theory since the middle of the nineteenth century has responded with denial, fascination, and occasionally something in between. First, there was the antiproduction movement, known initially as gothic revival and arts and crafts. This position sought to deny selecting and to maintain custom-craft artifacts as the basis for architecture. It continues to this day. Then there was its opposite, the complete commodification of architecture, in the literal form of mass-produced housing and in the more theoretical form of an early–twentieth-century art and architecture that had at least the appearance, if not the reality, of mass production.

More recently, there is the less familiar avenue of fusing mass production with custom context. This is the creative leap of vision from one context to another that led Picasso to see mass-produced bicycle parts transmogrified into a bull's head. Context engenders selection, then selection provokes the recomposition of the framework. Context and selection modify each other until neither appears as it once did, but both have combined to reinform one another in a new form. The capacity for re-envisioning is a promising vein for architecture to mine in the move toward an articulate craft of selecting.

Selecting is an act of design few architects care to acknowledge, yet if we are both reflective and honest, it is the act of design we all commit with the greatest frequency. Selecting is stealth architecture.

SELECTING

Shipley A standard school clock is transformed into an object of iconic significance through the simple yet deliberate act of framing. Elsewhere in the building, (on the opposite page) the seven materials used here fly in the face of conventional architectural wisdom suggesting no more than three materials in close proximity to one another. The reveal is especially helpful in erasing non-coplanar adjustments of dissimilar materials and construction inaccuracies. The double line in the unit heater surround provides the eye with a precise line to read and distracts from the inherent crudity of the wood/CMU joint.

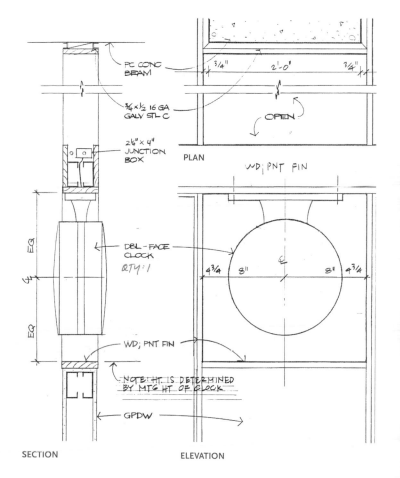

Ground face concrete block, Claridge slate blackboard and metal chalk tray, Fin-Ply, stained plywood, precast lintel, Duratherm mahogany window frames.

CF.   24 30 36 56 103 108 114 115 120 132 150 168

SELECTING

Chestnut Hill The half-inch reveals join the panels by holding them apart in much the same way that the transitional zone of this arcade joins the activity center to the academic world above by means of a gap. Heavy industrial steel sections provide armoring against wear and tear. Four frames continue the passage from the entry to the café beyond. They are furniture, free of the concrete ceiling above.

We intended the perforated metal screens to come from the McNichol's metals catalog; but the contractor found that the work could be fabricated more economically in his own shop. However, all the steel channels, angles, and bolts, were selected from standard manufactured shapes. Mail boxes, chalkboards, and light fixtures were also selected from catalogs.

CF. 60 76 114 164

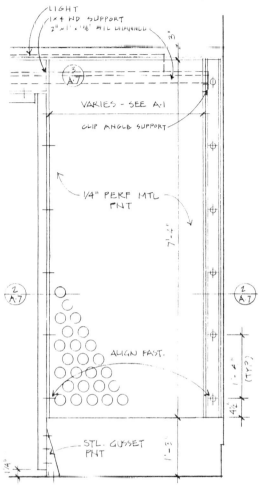

LIGHT
1x4 HD SUPPORT
2"x1'x1⅛' MTL CHANNEL

VARIES - SEE A·1

CLIP ANGLE SUPPORT

1/4" PERF MTL
PNT

7'-4"

ALIGN FAST.

1'-4"
(TYP)

4½"

STL. GUSSET
PNT

1'-3"

1/4"

PANEL ELEVATION

139

SELECTING

Kegler   An unusual confluence of circumstances led to an architectural ménage-à-trois, in which the architect was acting as the platonic third partner. The builder we suggested for this addition was a cabinetmaker who had built the wood screens for the Scott Residence and done other millwork for us. The client was a single mother—a painter and faux-finisher with whom we had worked on another project. Through this collaboration, they became a couple. The addition of self-finishing materials—stainless-steel tub liners, zinc shingles lining the tub wall, and Fin-Ply casework at the sink—represents a contrasting complement of self-finishing materials to the owner's craft of applied-finish surfaces.

TUB & SHOWER SHEET METAL DIAGRAM

Astra-Zinc, Fin-Ply, Endless Pool, Kohler Plumbing Fixtures.

SELECTING

Welles At a presentation to the third grade, one student expressed concern that the ceiling height would not be sufficient to accommodate his jump shot. We assured him that the trajectory of a basketball determined the sectional stepping of the gym. This joint further presented an opportunity to introduce natural lighting into a typically faceless space. The basilica form lets non-sporting events convert the space for their own purpose rather than causing you to feel as if you are compromising your program by having an assembly in a gym.

Kalwall translucent insulating panels, Tectum sound-absorbing panels, Duratherm maple and teak windows, galvanized metal ductwork, Porter Athletic Equipment Pro Strut basketball backboard model #224, Richstone United Glazed Products ground face CMU, Belden Brick Jewel blend A

CF. 37 72 112 118

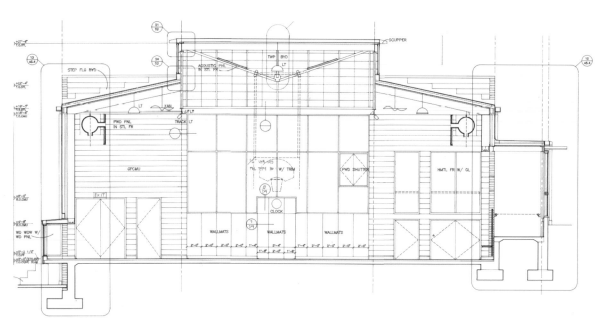

142

TRANSVERSE SECTION

143

SELECTING

Rider A & F   Cost can be a powerful editor. It establishes what is essential and therefore artful in a building. This is a simple two-story brick and block back-up structure, with a flat membrane roof and stucco walls. While budget constrained us to using standard windows, we were unconstrained in our determination to adapt the windows to our specific interest in minimizing profile. At times we consulted the manufacturers about the limitations of their products to find out if the windows could be installed backwards or upside down, thereby achieving the subtle variation in line weight we desired.

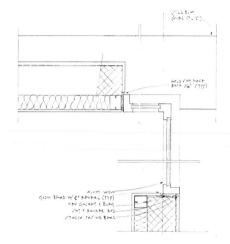

WINDOW PLAN

Aluminum trim and tees, stucco, interior veneer plaster, Kawneer aluminum window-framing system, brick

CF.   104 106 148

144

SLIPPING

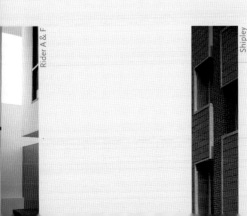

Rider A & F

Shipley

Keller

Sterling

E. Stroudsburg

Slipping is the sliding of planes or volumes relative to each other, be it one above and past another, one away and below another, or both moving transversely in the same plane but in opposite directions. If joining is about actual meeting and fusion, then slipping is about missing. The terms *meeting* and *slipping* are not opposites, for slipping conveys the idea of near miss, not complete miss. To constitute slipping, there must be a degree of closeness, of adjacency between the planes, volumes, or members competing for the same place. They must be seen as nearly aligned, or perhaps once aligned, to be understood as dislocated from a prior position.

In architecture, slipping is a method of construction and a compositional craft form of fairly ancient origin. Shingling, for example, depends on slipping to shed water. Starting at the bottom of a wall or roof, small shingles, be they wood, stone, large leaves, or bundles of thatch, slip above and to the side of those below; they never join. They always miss, slipping just past each other. Shingling is open enclosure. It is permeable to air yet sheds water by means of overlayment and gravity.

Entire elements and volumes of space in current architecture can slip relative to each other. Planes and volumes can be pulled apart by tension and slip away from each other, as in a room that contracts but leaves behind an exterior wall. Planes and volumes can also be pushed together by compression, moving toward and past each other, as when a shelf of space slides into the upper level of a large room. A third type of slipping is neither from nor toward but laterally about a transverse axis. Here the slipped elements remain in the same plane but relocate vertically relative to each other, as when the window to an intermediate stair landing slips vertically relative to the windows of an adjoining floor.

When slipping reveals the inner world of a building, it does so in stages, wall materials metamorphosing from thick stone to thin, uniform slate shingles to plate glass—from solid to transparent, natural to manufactured. Similarly, when slipping reveals the exterior world through a breach in the wall, it does not do so frontally. Rather, the connections between what is interior and exterior occur between planes, at glancing, fragmentary revelations in the faults between wall and volumetric linings and underlinings.

Developments in construction techniques have expanded the prospects for the use of slipping in exterior walls. Walls that fracture and slip past each other demand materials and ways to assemble them that ensure closure. The technological developments to meet these demands often come about in response to developments in architectural lining, such as the relatively recent emergence of durable elastic membranes, which are liners in their own right. These liners invite slipping. The introduction of these membranes for use in walls has freed the exterior wall from direct correlation to the interior wall and to its pattern of openings for windows and doors. In fact, to the extent that the exterior wall overlaps the boundaries of openings in the interior wall, performance is enhanced. The formal, compositional consequences are enormous.

An earlier, static world of alignment and union formally and materially dissolves, with just missing, not meeting, becoming the relationship of material and compositional desire.

SLIPPING

Rider A & F   A volumetric example of slipping occurs in the relationships between one- and two-story volumes and a connecting stair. One can understand a prior condition as stacked single story spaces, the second level slipping away in successive stages, revealing first an exterior wall that was once inside and is now a remnant left outside, and subsequently a two-story volume that was once layered single stories. Like most slipping, the end result is not neat, but rather misses adjoining volumes or surfaces. The corners never close, allowing a series of glancing views from a two-level stair through the open interior corner across the room to the open exterior corner beyond. From the programmatic slip of private administration zones into the public zones of the main hall, to the slip of partition next to volume, and down to the wood paneling, all details and volumes slide past each other.

CF.   104 106 144

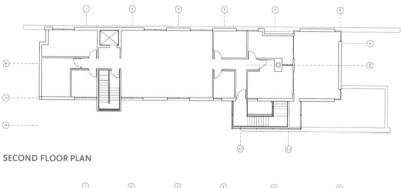

SECOND FLOOR PLAN

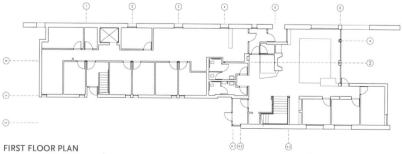

FIRST FLOOR PLAN

SLIPPING

Shipley The window misalignment is a large-scale instance of slipping. A stair provides the occasion for a landing—really a small floor—between building floors. To keep the sill-to-floor dimension constant, windows at stairs slip, or fault, about the transverse bearing walls. As the stair slips to an intermediate level, so does the window. The lead-coated copper trim provides an edge lining, visually highlighting the zipperlike slippage.

Shingled enclosures of roofs, and in this case walls, depend on overlap to create closure. The degree of overlap varies with material and angle of incline, but the basic principle is always the same: effective enclosure is created by layers of material, each unit slipping over and to the side of the unit below. We think of this wall as a "poor man's" pressure-equalized wall. The shingles are open to the air between their back surfaces and the sheathing, and restrained by exposed metal hooks.

CF. 24 30 36 56 103 108 114 115 120 132
     136 168

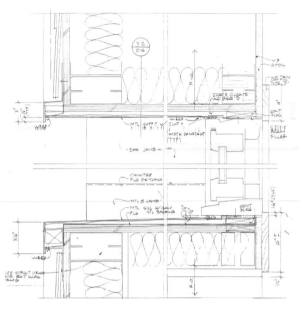

RECESSED WINDOW SILL/HEAD SECTION

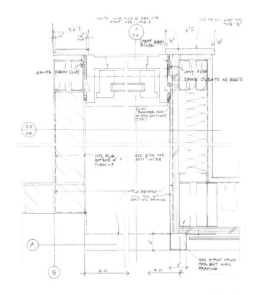

RECESSED WINDOW JAMBS PLAN

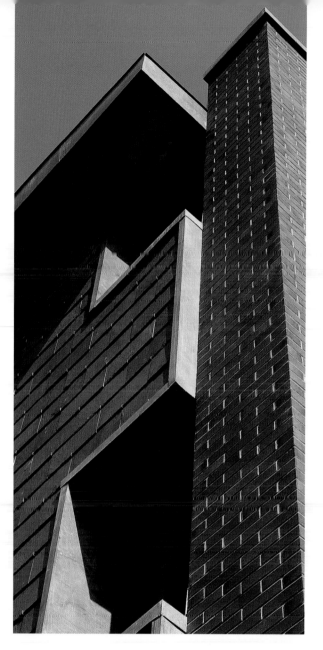

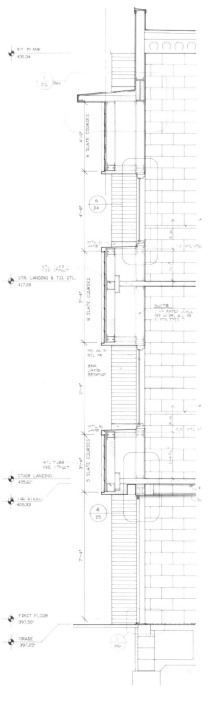

WALL SECTION

SLIPPING

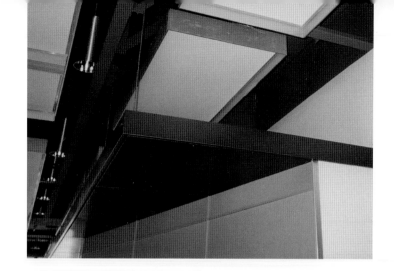

Keller This room is formed by a plane (ceiling) and a volume (room) moving toward and past each other. The wall and the space it shelters thrust into the lobby while the framed ceiling slips beyond, rendering boundaries negotiable. This is a large, square building footprint. The rooms at the center lack light. This glass soffit slips over the lobby wall, leaking natural light into a room buried deep within the building. It also provides a way to connect the inflected lobby wall to the orthogonal ceiling panels, closing the incompatible geometries of wall and ceiling. Both the lobby and the room beyond seem larger as a result of the transparent slipping of planes at the ceiling.

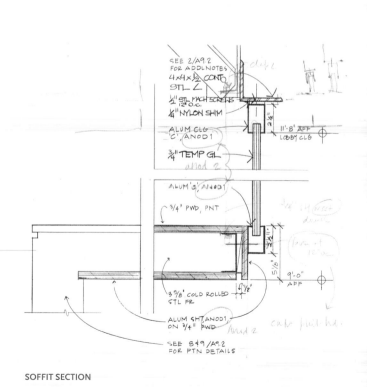

CF. 115 170

152

SOFFIT SECTION

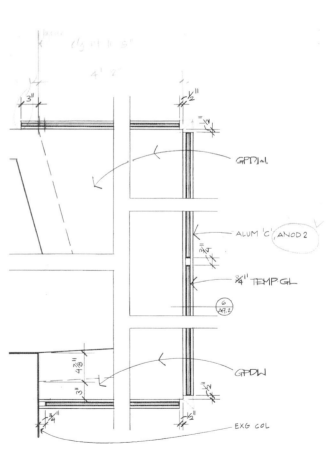

GPDJ al

ALUM 'C' ANOD 2

¾" TEMP. GL

6
A9.2

GPDW

EXG COL

REFLECTED CEILING SOFFIT PLAN

153

SLIPPING

Sterling   No one thought there could be a building site in this tiny courtyard. As we compressed the walls of the addition to turn and fit, they formed planes moving out of alignment with each other, revealing new edges and depth at the joints. This newfound depth is negotiated, location by location, by glancing views to and from the interior. As the addition compresses against an existing tower, it slips upward, past two elaborate stone arches, opening through the roof as a transverse shed dormer. The hidden window admits light at the fault, revealing and celebrating the void between new and old, between light and solid.

CF.   38 88 105 122 180

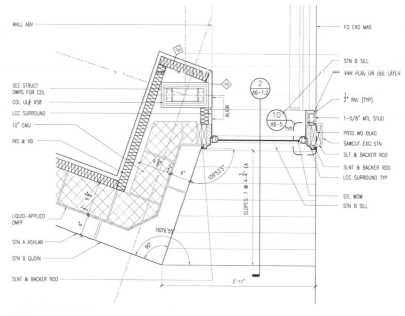

WALL ABV

FO EXG MAS

STN B SILL

VNR PLAS UN DBL LAYER

SEE STRUCT
DWRS FOR COL

COL UL# X58

LCC SURROUND

10" CMU

INS & VB

½" RVL (TYP)

1-5/8" MTL STUD

PRTD WD BLKG

SAWCUT EXG STN

SLT & BACKER ROD

SLNT & BACKER ROD

LCC SURROUND TYP

STL WDW

STN B SILL

LIQUID-APPLIED
DMPF

STN A ASHLAR

STN B QUOIN

SLNT & BACKER ROD

3'-11"

WINDOW SLOT PLAN DETAIL

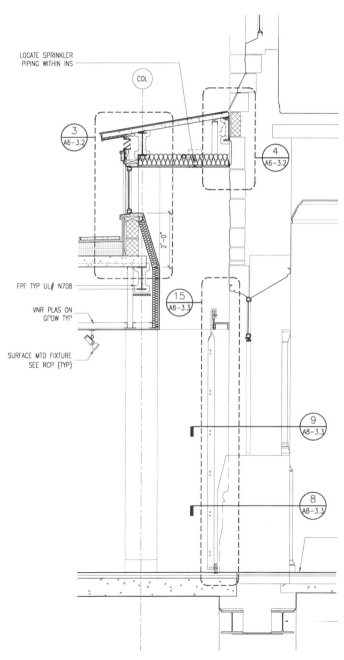

LOCATE SPRINKLER
PIPING WITHIN INS

COL

3
A6-3.2

4
A6-3.2

2'-0"

FPF TYP UL# N708

15
A8-3.3

VNR PLAS ON
GPDW TYP

SURFACE MTD FIXTURE
SEE RCP (TYP)

9
A8-3.3

8
A8-3.3

CLERESTORY SECTION

SLIPPING

E. Stroudsburg   Upon completion, a
secretary in the physical-plant
department took us out front,
pointed to the column penetrating
the entry wall and the irregular
window pattern about it, and huffed
"Explain that!" After a rambling
answer, she exclaimed, "Just what I
thought! You can't explain it." This
view of the University Center is a
provocation to the entire campus
with the seeming vulnerability of its
cladding. We think it desirable for
such a public building to be
extraordinary within the surrounding
population of ordinary brick
buildings. Due to the circumstantial
nature of the stone turning the
corner, the panels at the windows
miss and slip by each other. To avoid
biasing the facade to one side or the
other, the exposed edge of the stone
is alternated at every other joint. In
addition to provoking people's sense
of rightness about a building, the
overlap at the window protects the
joint between the window and the
back-up wall.

CF.   44 78 96 103 166

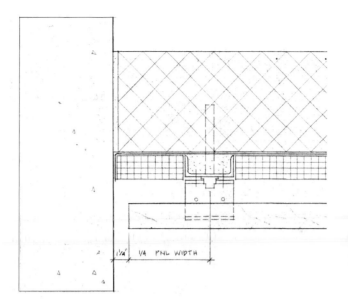

COLUMN/WALL PLAN

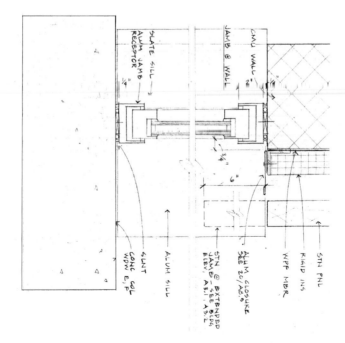

COLUMN/WINDOW PLAN

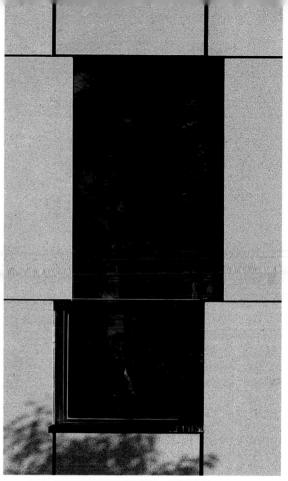

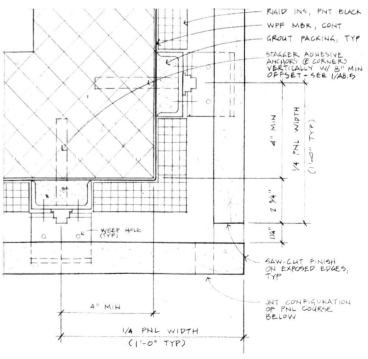

RIGID INS, PNT BLACK

WPF MBR, CONT

GROUT PACKING, TYP

STAGGER ADHESIVE
ANCHORS @ CORNERS
VERTICALLY W/ 8" MIN
OFFSET - SEE 1/A8.5

4" MIN

1/4 PNL WIDTH
(1'-0" TYP)

2 3/4"

1/4"

WEEP HOLE
(TYP)

SAW-CUT FINISH
ON EXPOSED EDGES,
TYP

JNT CONFIGURATION
OF PNL COURSE
BELOW

4" MIN

1/4 PNL WIDTH
(1'-0" TYP)

BUILDING CORNER PLAN

157

SLIPPING

Sykes We had been talking for a long time about trying to create the complementary inside-outside volumetric experience that was constructed here. The multipurpose room required a rather monumental, light-controlled box. To provide some scale to the enormous walls (both internally and externally), the corners were eroded, and the lining of construction was exposed. As the outer layer separates, the planes pulling apart, the underlining is revealed. This underlining is a framed, slate sheathed wall that shows itself behind a stone over mantel. The slate underlining faults in the same way, slipping past an even lighter and more transparent secondary underlining of glass.

CF. 37 42 70 98 104 115

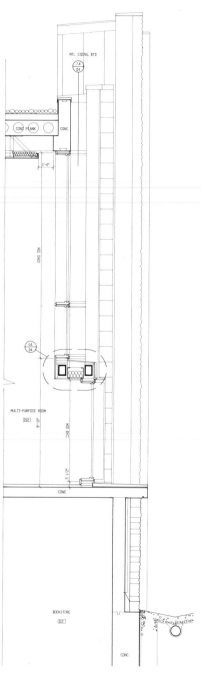

WINDOW SECTION

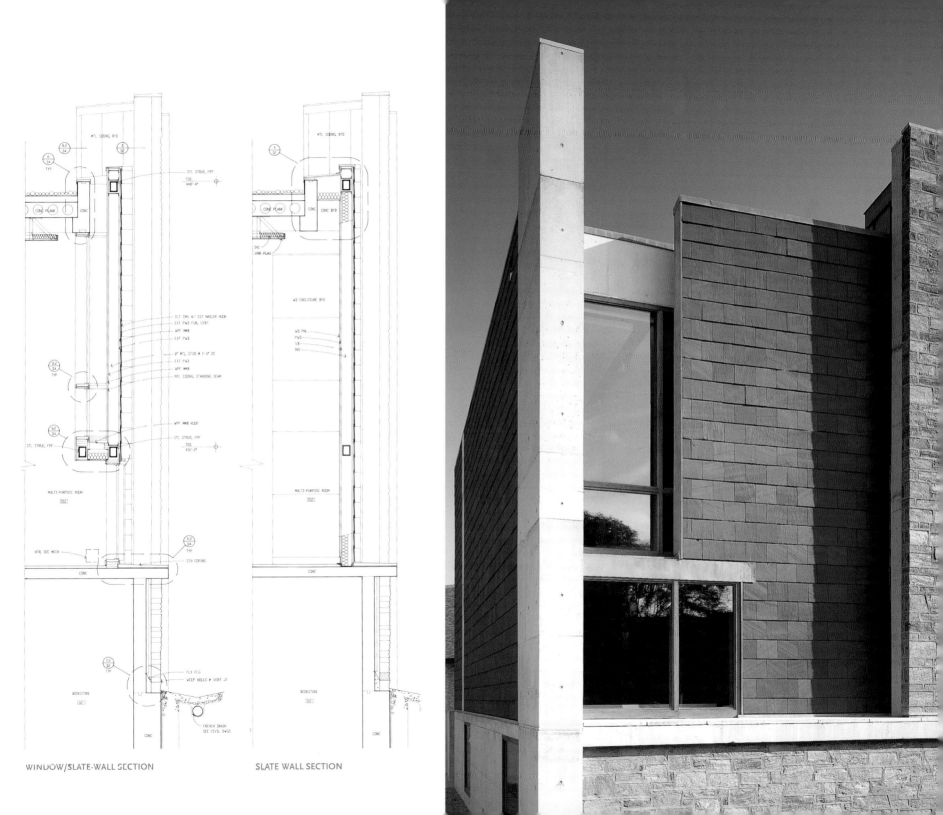

WINDOW/SLATE-WALL SECTION   SLATE WALL SECTION

WEAVING

Hamilton

Chestnut Hill

E. Stroudsburg

Shipley

Keller

Arden

Berkeley

Levine

Weaving is most often associated with textiles, but it is also relevant to architecture. It is a construct and a craft that can purposefully and aesthetically order building systems. Just as a thread can be pulled from a woven fabric and a new one inserted in its place, so too can building and urban systems be removed, replaced, or added when the whole is conceived as an exposed woven tapestry.

In its ancient usage, weaving creates surfaces and volumes by the regular interlacing of pliable strands—the warp and the woof—passing over and under each other at right angles. Friction at every joint enforces the structure of weaving. No material is completely inert, and under pressure from the environment, all materials deform. When deformed, many materials are elastic; they retain some memory of their prior state and will strain toward their original plane unless restrained. The bending of the strands, each of which wants to restore itself to a flat position, creates friction, between the threads at each overlap. This three-dimensional friction among strands above, below, and to each side, restrains the individual segments and forms the stable plane of a textile. In modern architectural usage, fasteners often provide the required friction in place of the deformation of the individual strands of material at work in textiles.

The building block, or cell, of a woven surface is the joint between overlapping materials. Weaving is in essence a continuous joint. In closely spaced weaving, the pattern of intersections becomes both visually and practically subservient to the plane or volume. Although the joint is normally an event of each physical consequence that it dominates our perception, in a densely woven form, the joint is transformed into a recessive contributor to the overall appearance of surface and shape. Weaving, however, can never be completely closed; it always has space between its strands. While the woven surface separates and contains, it breathes and connects. It is a scrim, a screen that is at once space and surface. Never quite a membrane, but part joint, part surface, part volume, part system, weaving is unique in architecture in being simultaneously open and closed.

The association of weaving with volume and system carries the craft into the deepest structures and largest scales of current architecture and urbanism. The integration of a large number of operating systems into buildings is a problem of relatively recent origin. Indoor plumbing has been common for less than 150 years; widespread electrification and elevators for vertical transportation are little more than a century old; air-conditioning and fire-suppression systems were novelties less than seventy-five years ago, and today, emergency power, door operators, and security, voice, and data transmission are part of the onslaught of systems that course through our buildings. The fundamental process and manner of conceiving architecture, however, has changed little. We still tend to organize program and space long before we integrate systems.

Viewed in relation to contemporary architecture, weaving is a conceptual and physical armature that accommodates the differential life spans of buildings and urban systems. At the same time that weaving provides for separation and the differential removal and replacement of elements, it composes and organizes single strands of material into a deliberately visual artifact, insisting upon repetition and pattern in its placement as purpose is translated into orderly artifice. Weaving celebrates the realization that permanence is no longer a prospect nor even a desire of architecture.

Rock Hall

Sterling

WEAVING

Hamilton The proposed infrastructure woven through these found and remembered structures introduces new patterns: one large, central, and public common at the scale of the campus and city; and eight small courtyards, outdoor rooms belonging to the eight college houses. All house quadrangles are accessible from Locust Walk, with trees, walks, and alleys reinforcing quadrangle identity. The hubs provide a visible house presence at the city frontages of Hamilton Village. They are academic storefronts, substituting program, social, and activity space for the retail fabric of the conventional city. The woof and warp of the tapestry is the urban structuring of site and adjacent streetscape, which retains and references prior histories while inverting the traditional walled separation of campus and city and fusing them into a transparent, new city-in-house/house-in-city.

SKETCH OF SMALL COURTYARD

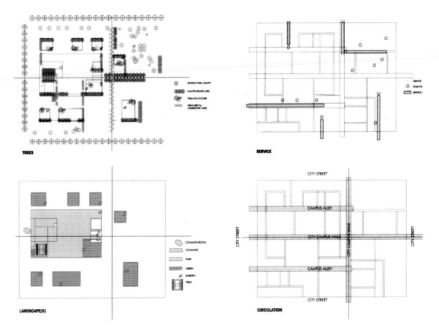

DIAGRAMS, CLOCKWISE FROM TOP LEFT: TREES, SERVICE, CIRCULATION, LANDSCAPE

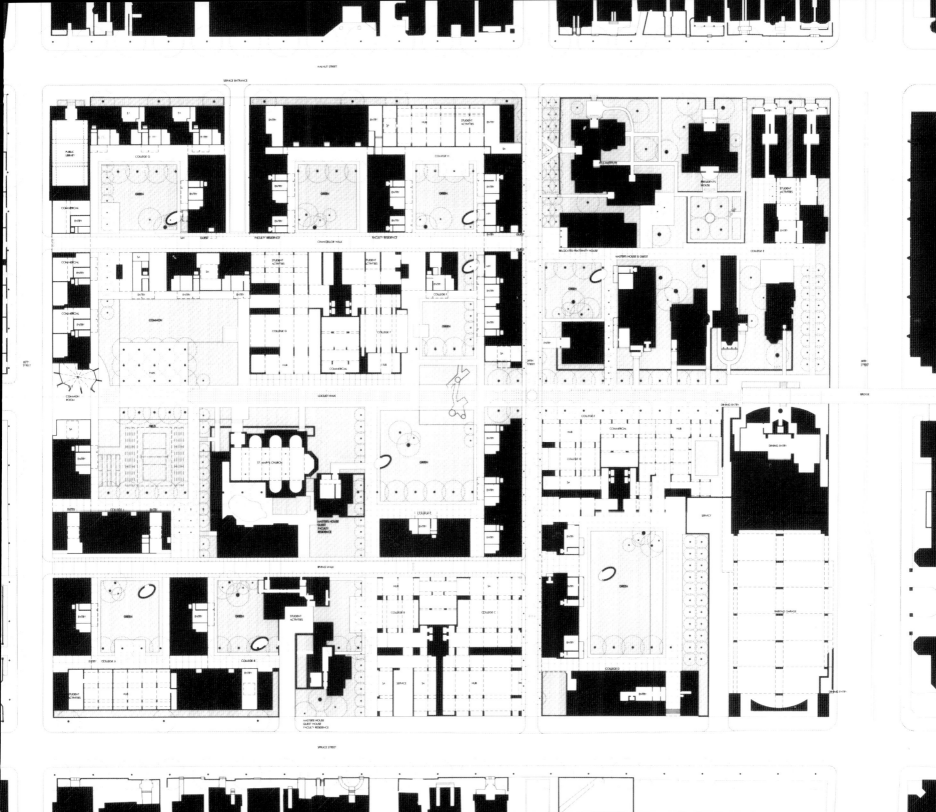

WEAVING

Chestnut Hill All paths open from Rome. In countless conversations at Rome's American Academy bar, the painter Al Held opened the spatial terrain of modernism to our then backward-looking eyes. His work suggested endless fields, space that you could climb into and be forever lost. A sister at this small Catholic women's college was one of the very few respondents to a mailing that announced the formation of our practice. She called to tell us it was beautiful but that they did not have any work. We met anyway. A year later, they had a project. The sisters wanted a profane space, a contrast to the sacred spaces and formal wood-paneled living rooms in the buildings above; yet the basement was a tangle of pipes, ductwork, and acoustic tile. One can choose to mask or ignore the everyday objects of necessity, but we were determined to create a system that would accept the undisciplined order of the existing systems.

CF. 60 76 114 138

REFLECTED CEILING PLAN

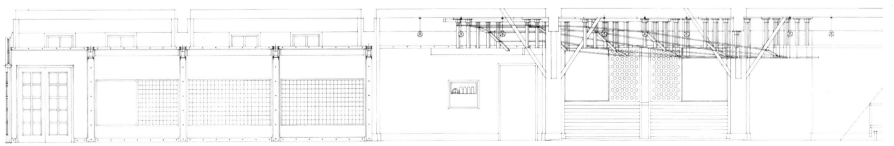

WEAVING

E. Stroudsburg   The building systems—steam piping, fire suppression, lighting, mechanical, voice, and data systems—were conceived as frames woven together. The infrastructure weaves in our other projects read more as ceiling layers within a space. Here the wood troughs are fundamental to the spatial dimension. All piping and ductwork were installed before the troughs were lifted into position. It would be an understatement to call the coordination "challenging," particularly given the confines of the trough and separate prime contractors. The building systems are only one aspect of the three-dimensional tapestry. The poured-in-place concrete frame, composed of directional piers and beams, is the datum through which the two-dimensional network of troughs weaves, integrating structure and system into a single tapestry.

CF.   44 78 96 103 156

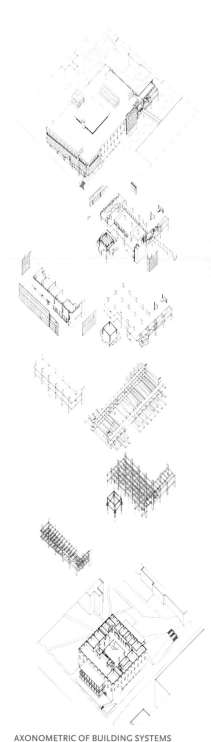

AXONOMETRIC OF BUILDING SYSTEMS

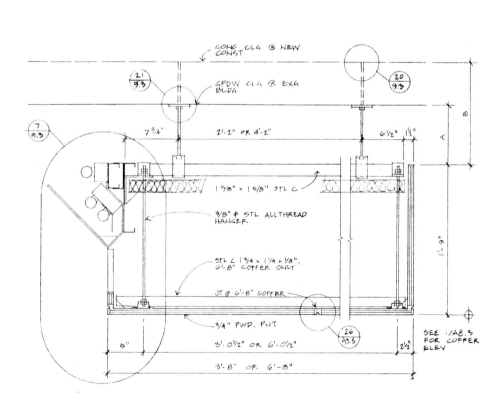

CONC CLG @ NEW CONST

GPDW CLG @ EXG BLDG

$\frac{21}{9.3}$

$\frac{20}{9.3}$

$\frac{7}{9.3}$

7 3/4"

2'-2" OR 4'-2"

6 1/2" 1 1/2"

B

A

1 5/8" x 1 5/8" STL C

3/8" Ø STL ALLTHREAD HANGER.

1'-9"

STL L 1 3/4 x 1 1/4 x 1/8", 6'-8" COFFER ONLY

JT @ 6'-8" COFFER

$\frac{26}{A9.3}$

3/4" PWD, PNT

5"

3'-0 1/2" OR 6'-0 1/2"

2 1/2"

SEE 1/A8.3 FOR COFFER ELEV

3'-8" OR 6'-8"

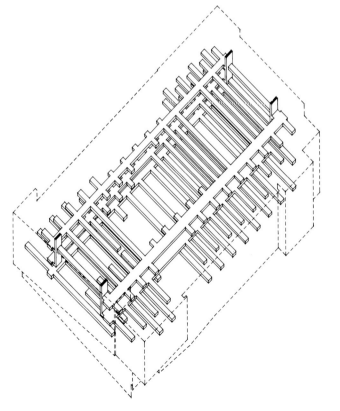

TROUGH SECTION

AXONOMETRIC OF MECHANICAL TROUGH SYSTEM

WEAVING

Shipley In our shop, there are no matters of lesser importance. At this new middle school, architecture is structure. It is fire protection, it is codes, it is equipment. It is all design. These systems are inseparable and intrinsic to the problem of designing a school. They are part of the education of children. Weaving provides a way to navigate what goes over and what goes under. We turn systems engineers into architects, and they turn us into engineers. Sometimes the engineers like the role reversal. Sometimes they go kicking and screaming into the world of woven systems. We have to trace every pipe and duct. We have to know how large it is, what it is made of, and how it turns. In this small building section, below a balcony walkway, all the building trades had to come to know and work with each other, while coinhabiting three feet four inches of common real estate. If one is not willing to become a mechanic, one should not become an architectural weaver.

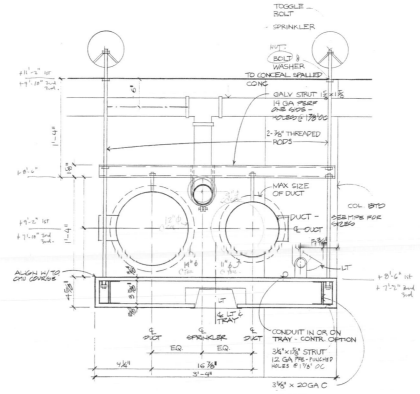

MECHANICAL TRAY SECTION

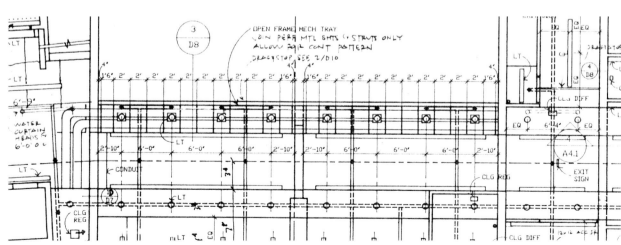

OPEN FRAME MECH TRAY
JOIN PERF MTL SHTS & STRUTS ONLY
ALLOW 2@12 CONT PATTERN
DRAFTSTOP SEE 2/D10

BRIDGE REFLECTED CEILING PLAN

WEAVING

Keller This lobby ran the risk of feeling too compressed, but by selectively opening the ceiling with infrastructural glimpses and by exaggerating the panel-lip edge, the space gains much-needed height. The reflective surface of the terrazzo floor further increases the virtual depth and throws light back to the ceiling. The materials that form the substance of this pattern are diverse. Aluminum edge angles form the actual structure and they outline the dominant visual structure: the voids penetrated by lights between the panels. The drywall panels are the last component. Fabriclike patches held in position by the threads of the aluminum angles. The electricians hated us that day. Our construction documents were clear, but they were running conduit across the lobby at diagonals. We had them rework the layout to a less distracting orthogonal, in concert with the panels.

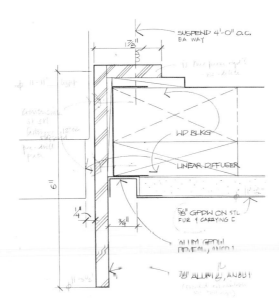

CEILING PANEL EDGE SECTION

CF.   115 152

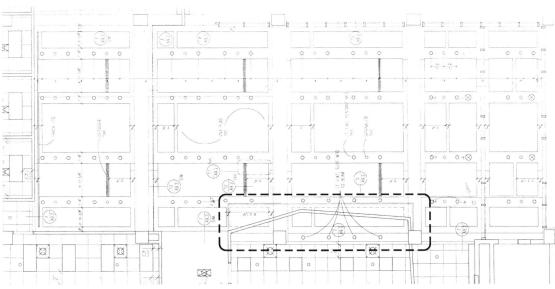

REFLECTED CEILING PLAN

WEAVING

Arden   We were hired by this client because we love infrastructure, construction, and process. Their first project, completed prior to our commission, was a study in surfaces that ignored the most important aspects of an existing building: the systems. Renovating this space for the theater was all about systems integration and construction.

The big move here—the act that overshadowed all others—was taking the structure away. First, new foundations were excavated by hand and poured. Next, steel columns were lowered through roof and floor penetrations to the new foundations. Demolition of the second floor was delayed so that it could be used as a sort of scaffolding for assembling the new long-span steel trusses. Finally, with the new trusses in place, the second floor and interior wood columns were removed to create one large, open space for performance.

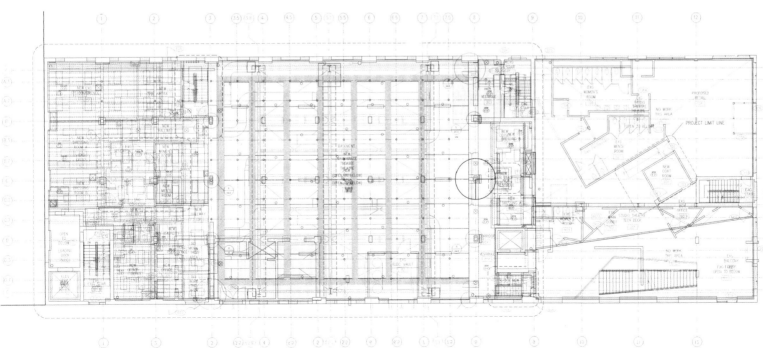

PLAN

WEAVING

Berkeley The blackened steel strapwork is a discovered order that holds two very different walls together: one of found masonry and the other of newly formed panels. This weave screens the usual infrastructural tangle of sprinkler piping, fire detection, and lighting in a mere six inches, which was all the clearance we had in this basement. Masking the artificial lighting diverts attention from the subterranean locale of this gathering space. Overlapping the strapping and light fixtures gains headroom as well. Careful coordination was required between trades that wanted nothing to do with each other. Fire-protection contractors, electricians, and metal fabricators all had to work in concert. Piping and conduit had to be installed to precise tolerances. The woven systems here are a compressed version of the elaborately carved wood ceiling by James Gamble Rogers in the dining hall located immediately upstairs.

CF.   14 16 37 54 62 80 105 115 130

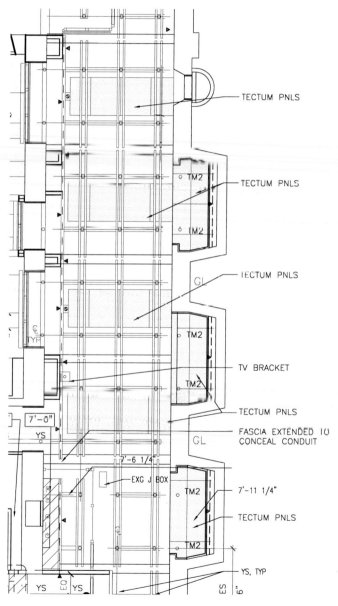

REFLECTED CEILING PLAN

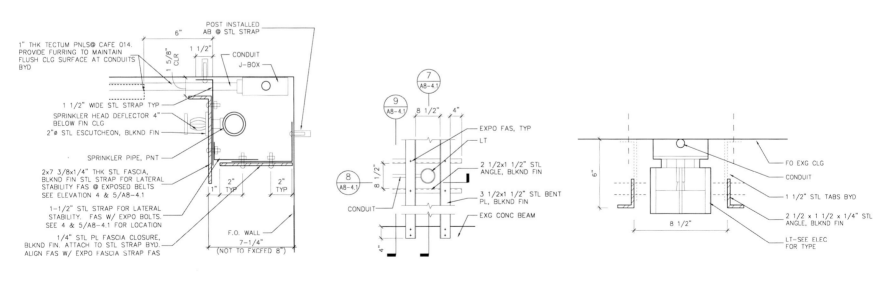

MECHANICAL FASCIA SECTION

1" THK TECTUM PNLS@ CAFE 014.
PROVIDE FURRING TO MAINTAIN
FLUSH CLG SURFACE AT CONDUITS
BYD

POST INSTALLED
AB @ STL STRAP

6"

1 5/8" CLR

1 1/2"

CONDUIT
J-BOX

1 1/2" WIDE STL STRAP TYP

SPRINKLER HEAD DEFLECTOR 4"
BELOW FIN CLG

2"ø STL ESCUTCHEON, BLKND FIN

SPRINKLER PIPE, PNT

2x7 3/8x1/4" THK STL FASCIA,
BLKND FIN STL STRAP FOR LATERAL
STABILITY FAS @ EXPOSED BELTS
SEE ELEVATION 4 & 5/A8-4.1

1-1/2" STL STRAP FOR LATERAL
STABILITY. FAS W/ EXPO BOLTS.
SEE 4 & 5/A8-4.1 FOR LOCATION

1/4" STL PL FASCIA CLOSURE,
BLKND FIN. ATTACH TO STL STRAP BYD.
ALIGN FAS W/ EXPO FASCIA STRAP FAS

1" TYP
2" TYP
2" TYP

F.O. WALL
7-1/4"
(NOT TO EXCEED 8")

STRAPWORK PLAN

7
A8-4.1

9
A8-4.1

8 1/2"   4"

8
A8-4.1

8 1/2"

CONDUIT

4"

EXPO FAS, TYP

LT

2 1/2x1 1/2" STL
ANGLE, BLKND FIN

3 1/2x1 1/2" STL BENT
PL, BLKND FIN

EXG CONC BEAM

STRAPWORK SECTION

6"

8 1/2"

FO EXG CLG

CONDUIT

1 1/2" STL TABS BYD

2 1/2 x 1 1/2 x 1/4" STL
ANGLE, BLKND FIN

LT-SEE ELEC
FOR TYPE

WEAVING

Levine The School of Engineering wanted the building's approach to construction to be a symbol of itself. There was enthusiastic support for the pressure-equalized curtain wall, but subsequently, there was also concern for seeking an approach sensitive to the rest of the aged-brick campus. By knitting the curtain wall, with the brick, a detail was created that allowed the client to fully embrace the design. Large stone units reinforce vulnerable corners and interlock themselves with the brick field. Where the new glass building joins the existing masonry complex, the brick weaves its way, zipperlike, into the glass curtain wall. This is an important detail for the university. It is the moment of negotiation between the turn-of-the-century structures and the twentieth-century glass curtain wall.

To keep the cantilevered brick from interfering with the curtain wall, a concrete shearwall is used as the supporting structure.

CF. 64 126

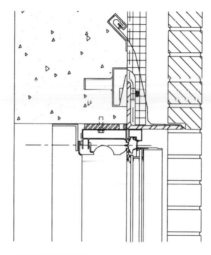

BRICK LINTEL HEAD

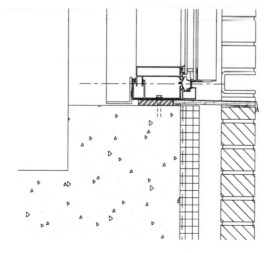

BRICK LINTEL SILL

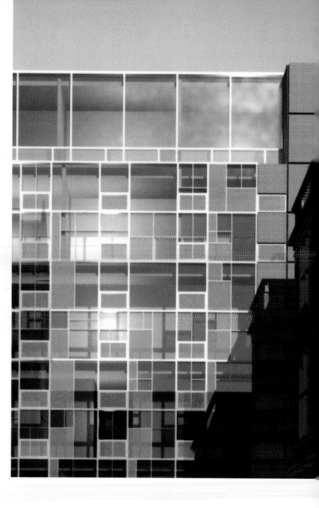

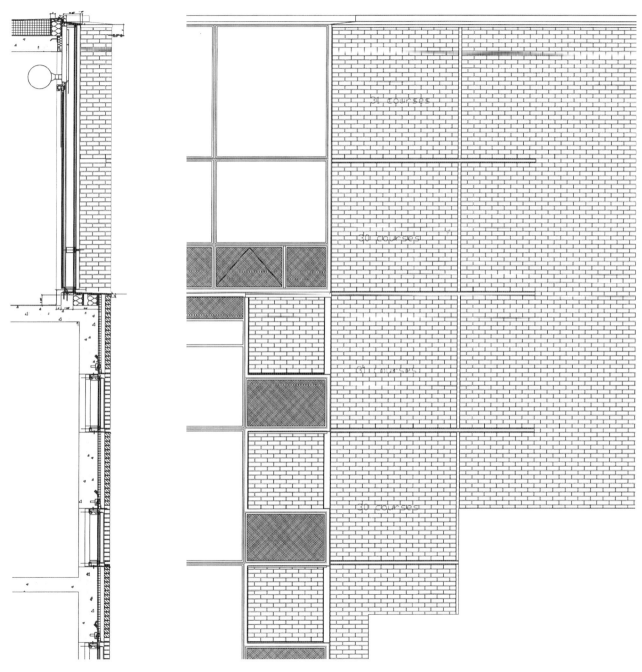

31 courses

30 courses

31 courses

30 courses

BRICK/CURTAIN WALL SECTION   WEST ELEVATION

WEAVING

Rock Hall What is the depth of the imitative versus the authentic? One is a fictive invention, and the other is a fiction derived from necessity. In this auditorium, we use the idea of the room as a musical instrument; the depth of the sound box is represented in the depth of the weave. The metaphor is one of tectonic reality and is drawn from the program. The acoustical requirement of fifty percent absorptive and fifty percent reflective surfaces led to a proscenium that exploits the depth and lightness offered by flat panels. It is a solution which balances the question of imitation versus invention.

The strands in this textile are typically six-inch-wide plywood strips with a two-foot-wide central panel. During design, we built a full-scale panel with a small millworker to test the ability of the plywood to bend and for the necessity of fasteners at points of overlap. An adjustable metal superstructure supports the woven wood panels.

CF. 48

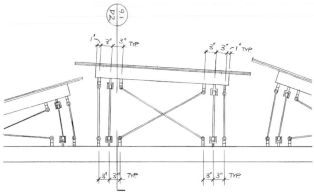

PROSCENIUM PANEL PLAN

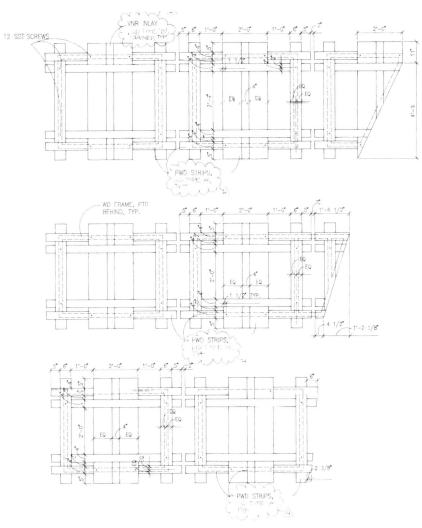

PROSCENIUM PANEL ELEVATIONS

WEAVING

Sterling   We love direct challenges
from our architectural ancestors. The
blunter the challenge, the better. Our
addition comes squarely up against
the stone walls and elaborate
windows of James Gamble Rogers's
1930s structure. We sought direct
competition with the original
wrought-iron metalwork by using
stainless-steel and bronze rods and
straps, but the new gates in no way
cancel the stone craft against which
they are juxtaposed. The old stone
carving and the new metal gates,
while of different ages, are equal crafts.

The fabricator really rose to the task.
Consider that every pair of bends in
the stainless-steel bar—out, then
back to vertical again—had to be
made in precisely the right location
so as to intersect the three-quarter-
inch bronze bar where the button-
head fastener, passing through a
predrilled hole, would lie flat against
it. When asked what he had worked
on before these gates, he replied,
"Something for the space shuttle."

CF.   38 88 105 122 154

180

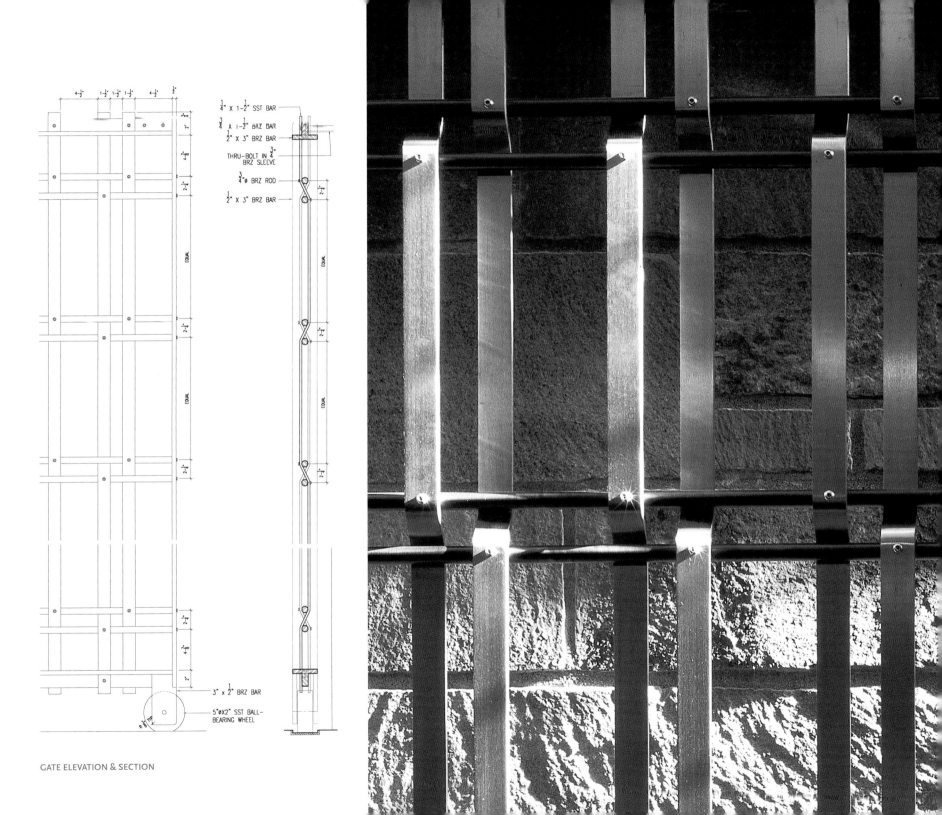

GATE ELEVATION & SECTION

1/4" X 1-1/2" SST BAR

3/4" X 1-1/2" BRZ BAR

1/2" X 3" BRZ BAR

THRU-BOLT IN 3/4"
BRZ SLEEVE

3/4"ø BRZ ROD

1/2" X 3" BRZ BAR

3" X 1/2" BRZ BAR

5"øX2" SST BALL-
BEARING WHEEL

Chestnut Hill 1987

Scott 1988

KTA 1989

Greenberg

Shapiro

Stufano

Allingham 1990

Kegler 1991

Villanova

Rider S & T 1992

ESP

Shipley 1993

E. Stroudsburg

Rider A & F

Rock Hall 1995

INDEX

1996   1997   1999   2000   2001   2002

Keller   Welles   Armfield   Aiden   Berkeley   Chiller   Hamilton   E & O   Walker   Marks   Sterling   Stafford   Levine

183

Student Activity Center
Chestnut Hill College
1987

Over the years these basements
became the inadequate home to a
variety of programs not anticipated
in the 1920s. The firm was asked to
design a centralized space for
student activities in the basement
connecting two Romanesque-revival
mixed-use buildings. The core of the
project entirely reprogrammed the
basement for more contemporary
student uses. In total, the basement
complex not only links separate
wings and buildings internally, but it
also affords students a variety of
places to relax, study, and socialize.

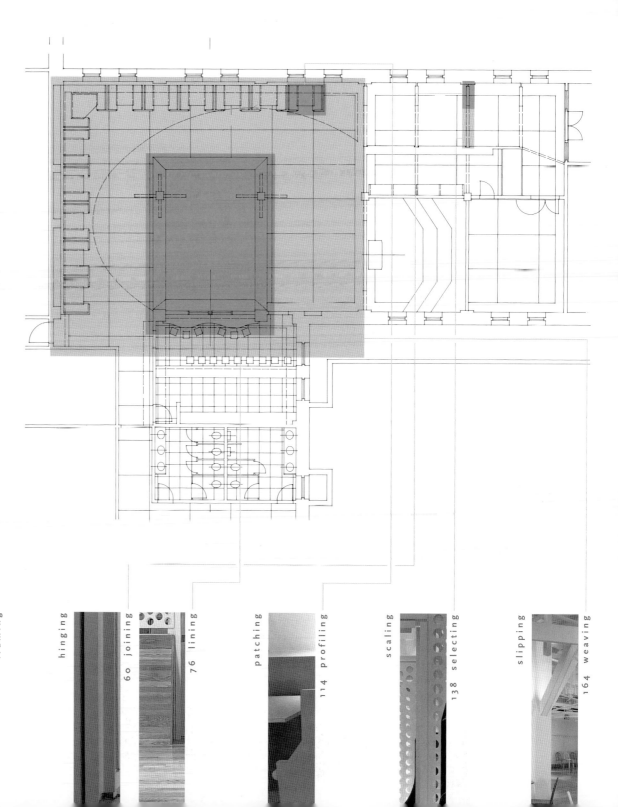

framing

hinging

60 joining

76 lining

patching

114 profiling

scaling

138 selecting

slipping

164 weaving

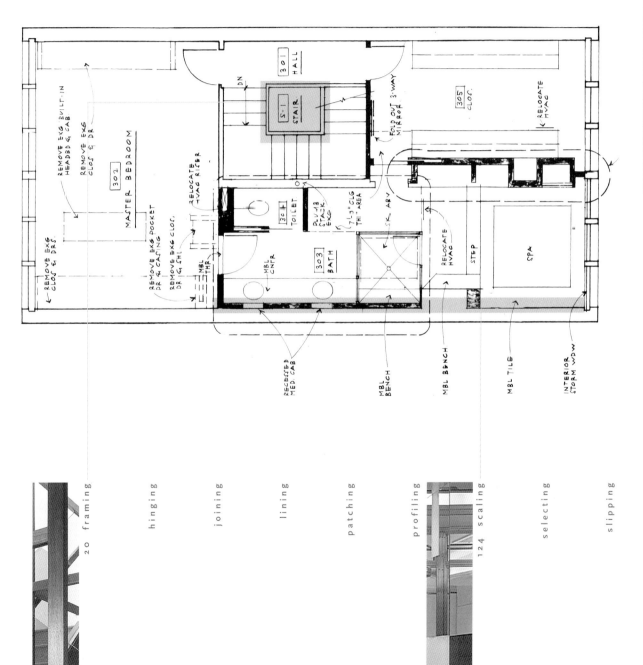

The owner's program required renovations to the interior stair, to open the core of the house visually and spatially. The new stair was inserted into the existing well using a mahogany structure and sliding screens to open and close the adjacent spaces. The new bathroom includes a separate toilet compartment, shower, whirlpool bath, and full media technology.

20 framing   hinging   joining   lining   patching   profiling   124 scaling   selecting   slipping   weaving

When we started our office
seventeen years ago, we needed to
balance the minimal number of
commissions we had with our desire
to outfit an office. Therefore, editing
and simplicity led us to select
materials and finishes that expressed
the essence of architecture to us.

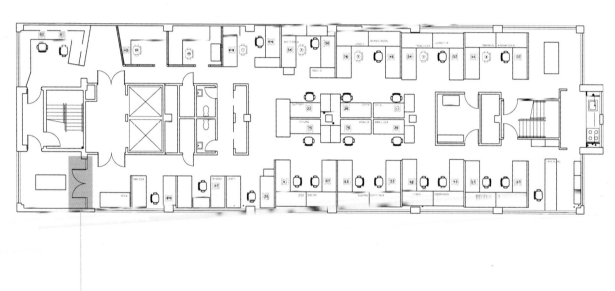

186

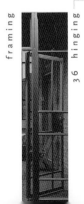

framing   36 hinging   joining   lining   patching   profiling   scaling   selecting   slipping   weaving

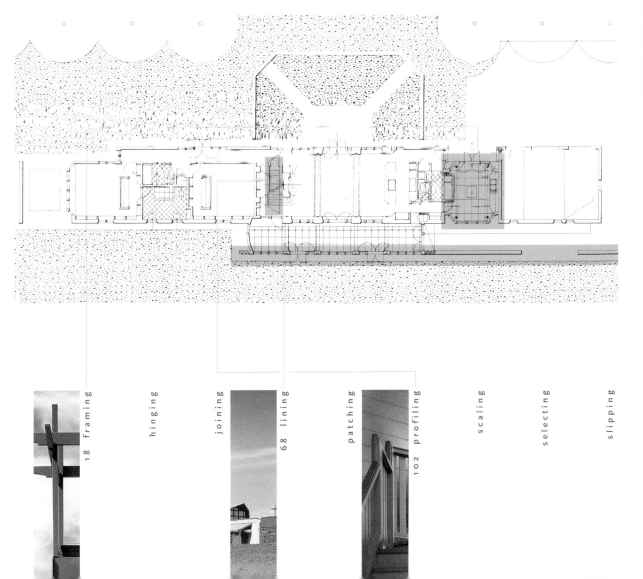

18 framing   hinging   joining   68 lining   patching   102 profiling   scaling   selecting   slipping   weaving

Located on a crest to the rear of a meadow, the overall concept of the wall is reinforced by vernacular shed imagery combined with a series of roof structures. The shed roof literally and figuratively reinforces the wall. The largest volume on the shed roof is the great room hood, at once joined to and emerging from the lower horizontal volume. The studio, behind the wall, has a special relationship to the landscape, which was required by the clients, one of whom is a landscape designer. The studio wall is faceted and cut to form a sculptural whole within the shed structure.

The site is a typical New Jersey subdivision of lots arranged along curving streets. The central problem of conventional suburban homes is their failure to define public, private, and service realms within the suburban landscape. Our aim was to provide a clear hierarchy of exterior space and land use. Bending the plan establishes a public face to the street and separates that realm from the private and service areas to the rear. Internally, the house is arranged into a linear, narrative sequence of rooms framed by the overhanging outdoor spaces of patio and porte cochere at the extreme ends of the home.

framing   40 hinging   joining   74 lining   patching   102 114 profiling   scaling   selecting   slipping   weaving

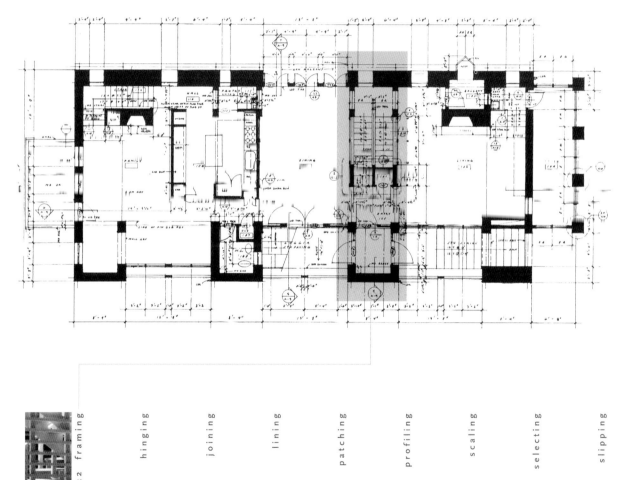

22 framing   hinging   joining   lining   patching   profiling   scaling   selecting   slipping   weaving

Four pairs of parallel walls entering the hillside establish the relationship of house to landscape. These revetments appear as towers on the west riverfront and culminate in large dormers above a buttressed wall to the east side. On the river side, U-shaped towers provide a stable bearing support for the girders that frame the house. On the side opposite, a buttressed wall of diminishing thickness rises in three tiers, from the base to the top floor, providing a visual as well as an actual counterthrust to the towers.

Allingham Summer Residence
1990

Located in Maryland on a two-acre
site overlooking the Chesapeake Bay,
this residence used a consistent
palette of wood inside and out. The
frame is an exposed-wood skeleton,
infilled with wood window frames
and panels. The first floor contains
two porches and a combined living,
dining, and kitchen area. A children's
bedroom with three bunks, a guest
bedroom, and one bathroom are
found on the second floor. The master
bedroom suite perches at the upper-
most level, with views across the bay.

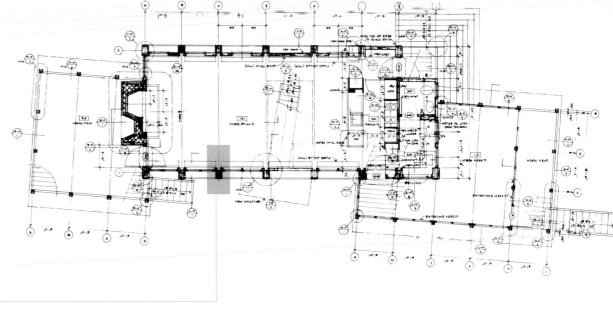

32 framing   hinging   joining   lining   patching   profiling   scaling   selecting   slipping   weaving

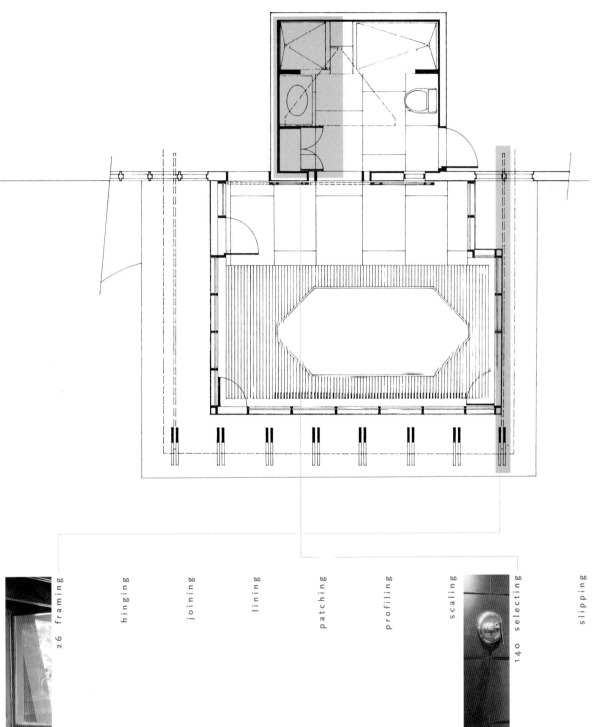

26 framing   hinging   joining   lining   patching   profiling   scaling   140 selecting   slipping   weaving

Formerly a chicken coop, this project includes an addition for a stationary lap pool with a bathroom/dressing room in an adjoining renovated space. The frame of the pool house is mahogany, with stainless steel connections. Green Finland plywood completes the underside of the lap-pool ceiling. The pool, tub, and shower pans are stainless steel. A redwood floor forms the pool house deck. Slate flooring extends from the edge of the pool into the bathroom and forms the tub and shower base. Yellow Fin-Ply walls line the bathroom enclosure.

Campus Entrance
Villanova University
1991

Once a rural road connecting
Philadelphia and Lancaster, this road
was eventually widened to become a
four-lane highway. Because the
university lacked space on the older,
traditional campus to the north of
Lancaster Avenue, it had to devote a
large tract of land to the south to
campus parking and student
residences. Students therefore have
to cross Lancaster Avenue to get to
the main campus. Given the traffic
increases, the university, township,
and the Pennsylvania Department of
Transportation agreed to address the
confluence of cars and people at this
intersection with a pedestrian
underpass.

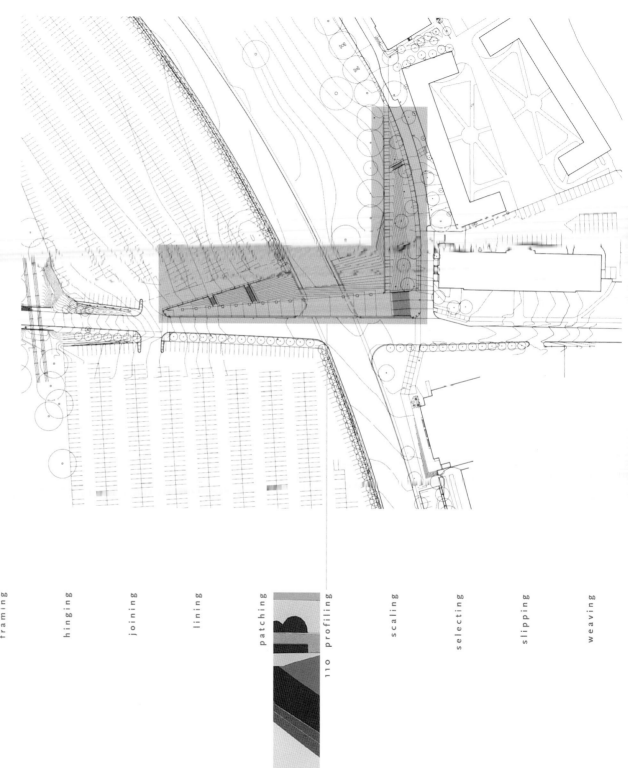

framing   hinging   joining   lining   patching   110 profiling   scaling   selecting   slipping   weaving

192

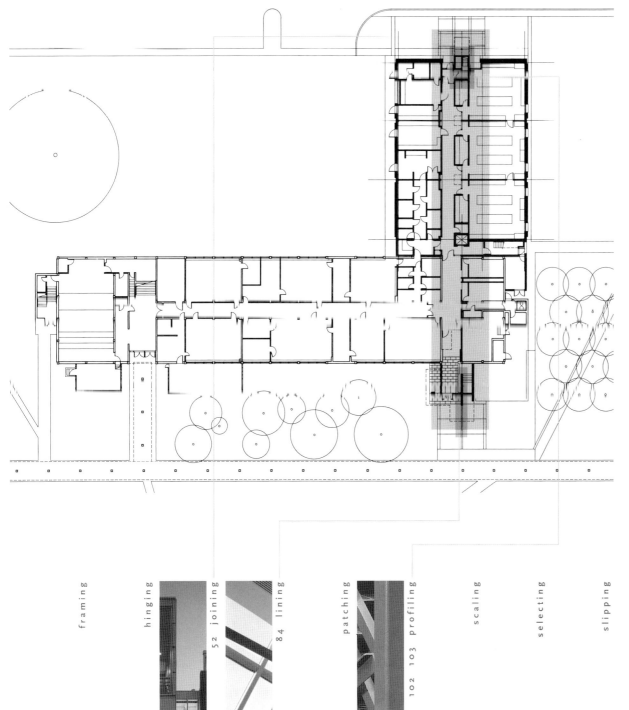

One of four structures forming the main academic quadrangle, this project includes two phases: an addition, followed by a renovation. The addition is inserted through the existing structure to provide a new main entrance on the quadrangle and a sequence of laboratories along the central corridor, which culminates in a rear stair and entry. During the second phase renovation, a new stair tower was added to provide the quadrangle with a much needed focal point.

framing hinging 52 joining 84 lining patching 102 103 profiling scaling selecting slipping weaving

Designed by John Haviland, Eastern
State Penitentiary is the prototypical
example of the centrally organized
prison. Currently a ruin, the first
three phases of a planned four-phase
project were completed to survey,
assess, plan, and implement
stabilization procedures. The fourth
phase identified new uses for the
landmark.

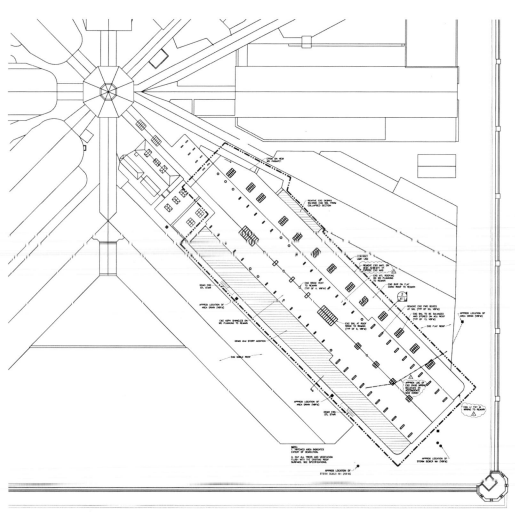

framing   36 hinging   joining   82 lining   patching   profiling   scaling   selecting   slipping   weaving

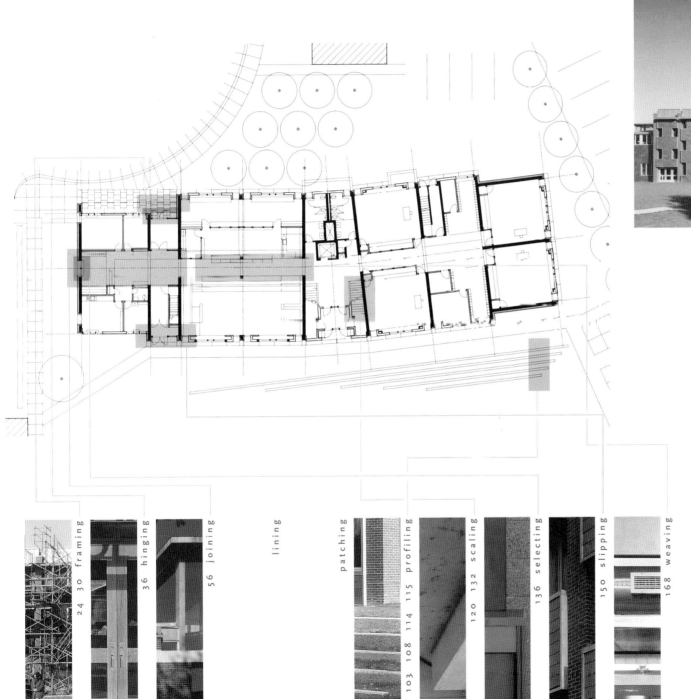

The program criteria centered on flexibility and the desire to gather classes together for cross-teaching arrangements. This yielded clusters of classrooms surrounding a shared group area. The new middle school is intended to be part of the educational experience. Reinforcing architectural understanding to young students, the mechanical and structural systems are organized and layered to code the building and the methods of its construction. The palette consists of durable self-finishing materials that age with a graceful patina.

24 30 framing
36 hinging
56 joining
lining
patching
103 108 114 115 profiling
120 132 scaling
136 selecting
150 slipping
168 weaving

195

University Center
East Stroudsburg University
1993

The existing University Center is a
square building located between the
original academic campus to the
west and the principal residential
quadrangle to the east. This project
added to both the north and south
sides of the existing structure,
transforming it from object into
bridge (both metaphorical and
literal) connecting the academic and
residential quadrants. Reinforcing
this connection, many fragments of
the existing building are left as
evidence of the original structure,
including an appropriation of the
steel frame, exterior brick walls, and
interior walls of concrete masonry.

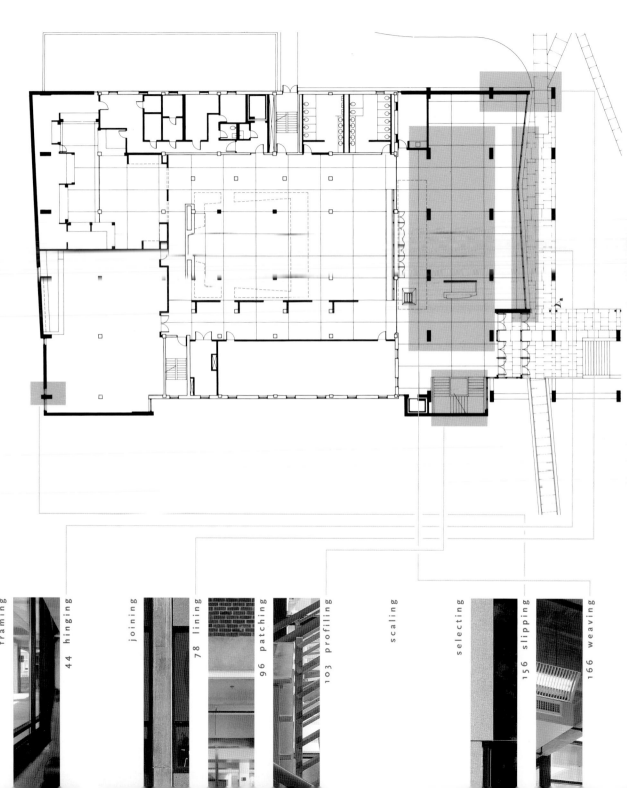

framing   44 hinging   joining   78 lining   96 patching   103 profiling   scaling   selecting   156 slipping   166 weaving

This project is the site hyphen between two very large adjoining buildings. Together the three buildings unite this area of campus with the academic quadrangle. As the administrative offices emerge against the main stair and welcoming room, they overlap the open volume: the second-floor conference room and the dean's office extend into this space, forming a single height reception area below and allowing views across the welcoming room out to the campus. The spatial sequence from enclosed office block to welcoming room culminates with the garden as implied room.

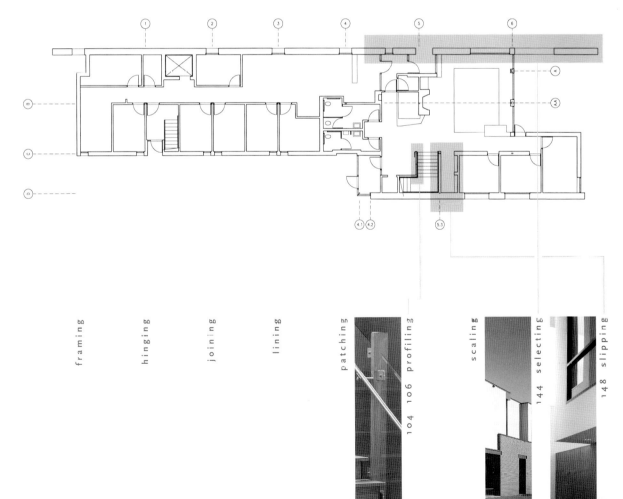

framing

hinging

joining

lining

patching

104 106 profiling

scaling

144 selecting

148 slipping

weaving

197

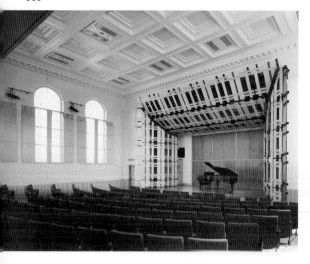

The primary purpose of this interior renovation was the creation of a chamber music recital hall for teaching and public-performance functions. In addition, a music library, administrative offices, faculty studios, classrooms, practice rooms, and computerized-music laboratories completed the program directives. Working within the constraints of the existing building envelope and neoclassical facade, we sought to strengthen the architectural characteristics and accommodate the program with a series of insertions particular to each space and purpose.

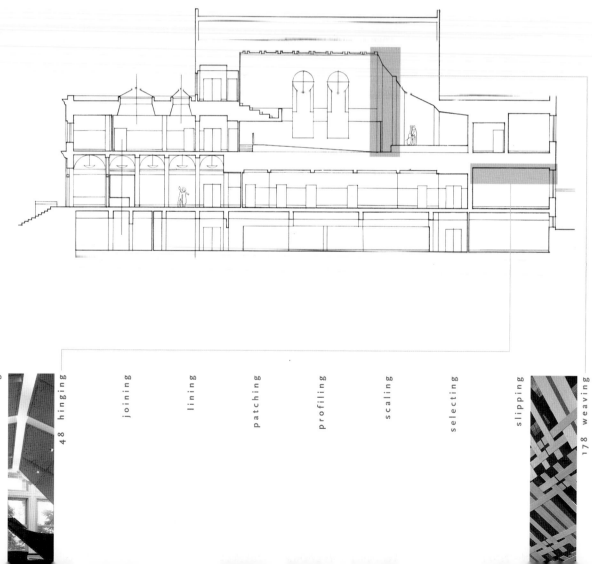

framing   48 hinging   joining   lining   patching   profiling   scaling   selecting   slipping   178 weaving

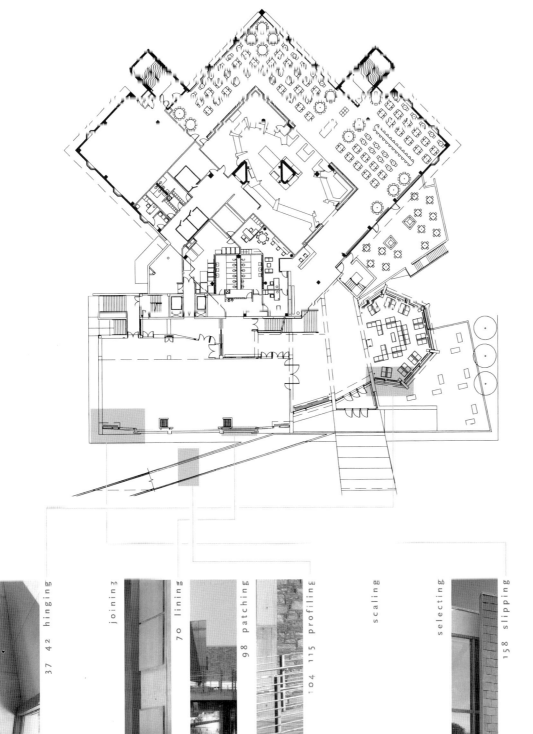

Recalling the academic quad's masonry, the new stone wall masks the addition's multipurpose facility, acts as a reminder of the collegiate gothic buildings to the northeast, and is intended to knit the campus rift created by Rosedale Avenue. The reconfigured structure corrects the confusing entry and corridor layout in the existing building with a centralized circulation pattern. A main stair and atrium orient occupants looking for a landmark between floors and new spaces, welcome visitors with natural light, and connect back to the outdoors through terrace extensions and broad, open window areas.

framing
37 42 hinging
joining
70 lining
98 patching
104 115 profiling
scaling
selecting
158 slipping
weaving

199

Keller Building
Pennsylvania State University
1995

With a new program to squeeze into
this renovation, the large lobby had
to be reduced. To maintain the
expansive nature of the original
space, a mullionless, partially
translucent glass partition was
added across the back of the lobby to
define space for Continuing
Education. A large mural along the
back wall of this open office area,
visible through the glass wall,
maintains the sense of expansion
beyond the new, smaller lobby.
Offices for four colleges, along with
classrooms, form the new building
program.

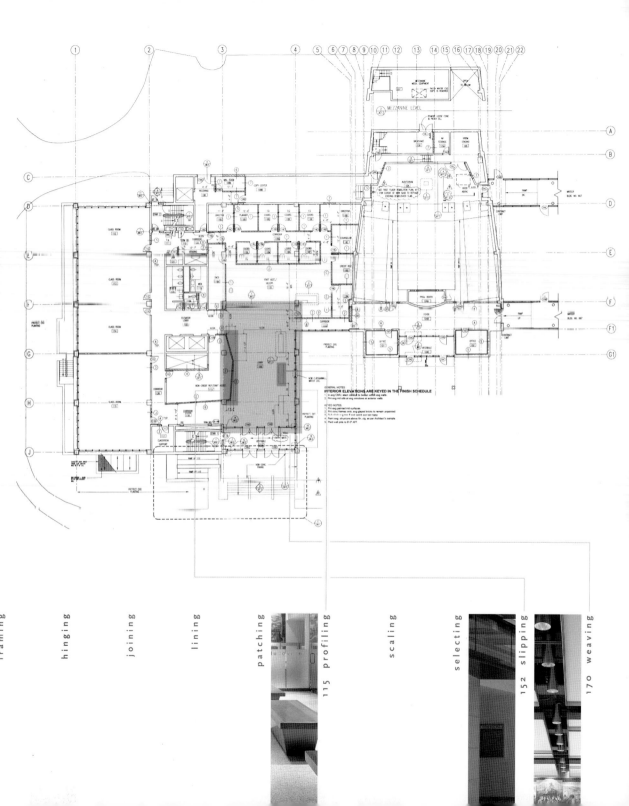

framing   hinging   joining   lining   patching   115 profiling   scaling   selecting   152 slipping   170 weaving

200

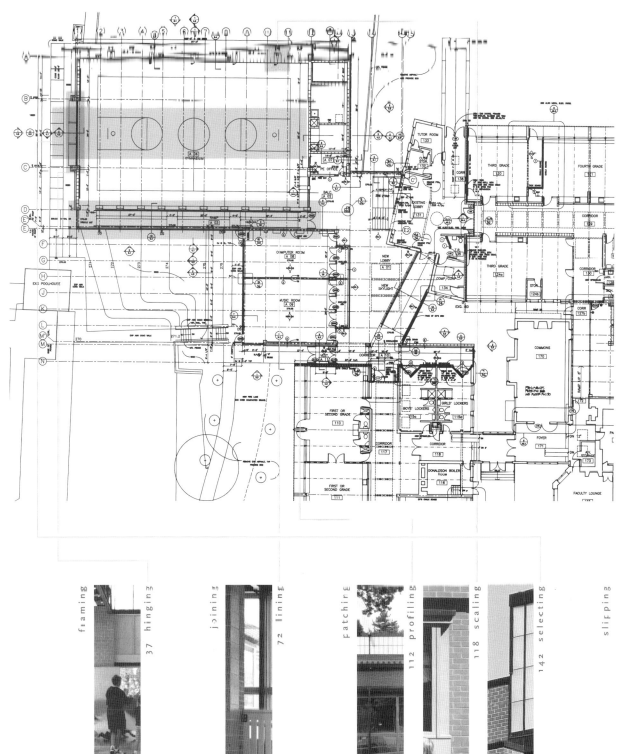

The program criteria centered on the need for flexibility in serving different functions and age groups. The activity center was intended to serve primarily as a meeting space for school assemblies and informal performances for the lower school. Secondarily, the space needed to serve as a gym for the lower school and an athletic space for middle school intramural sports. While the secondary uses determine the size of the space, the primary need for a room rather than a gym led to the selection of a warm palette of ground-faced concrete block and brick bearing masonry, with mahogany infill windows.

framing

37 hinging

joining

72 lining

fatchire

112 profiling

scaling

118 scaling

142 selecting

slipping

weaving

Armfield Hall
Woodberry Forest School
1997

The new Armfield Hall links two
existing buildings at a boy's
preparatory school in central
Virginia, and forms a humanities
courtyard, which opens off the
central lawn. It houses fifteen new
classrooms, offices, a lecture room,
and a faculty lounge. We sought
authenticity in the materials,
proportions, and composition while
incorporating contemporary
construction techniques. The
exterior walls are brick, with a
pattern of open-head joints following
rainscreen principles.

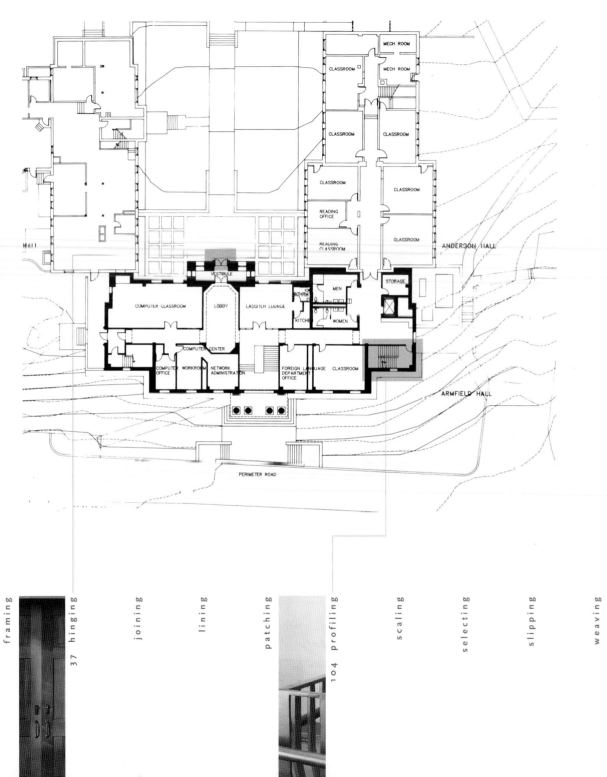

framing   37 hinging   joining   lining   patching   104 profiling   scaling   selecting   slipping   weaving

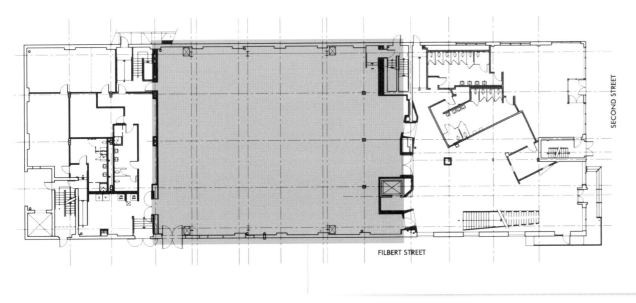

FILBERT STREET

SECOND STREET

The guiding principle here was to yield a fully flexible space defined by the systems and the character of the existing warehouse building. The result is a space that serves as a background for theater; the plays define the foreground. To create the required flexibility, an entirely new structural system was designed to support the existing walls and roof and to allow the removal of the interior structure. The new structure was inserted into the existing building while the Arden continued to operate and present productions in an adjacent theater.

framing   hinging   joining   lining   patching   profiling   scaling   selecting   slipping   weaving

203

Like all buildings, Berkeley began to
change the day it was completed. In
addition to changes driven by
program, taste, and regulation,
weather and human wear have been
relentless. The completed alterations
and renovations at Berkeley College
strive to elevate the design dialogue
about interventions in historic
structures. Unlike older cultures,
there is an increasing unease about
change within historic American
structures. The alterations at
Berkeley—part art, part history, part
science—recognize architecture as
an intergenerational event and seek
a living, as opposed to a museum
relationship, with the past.

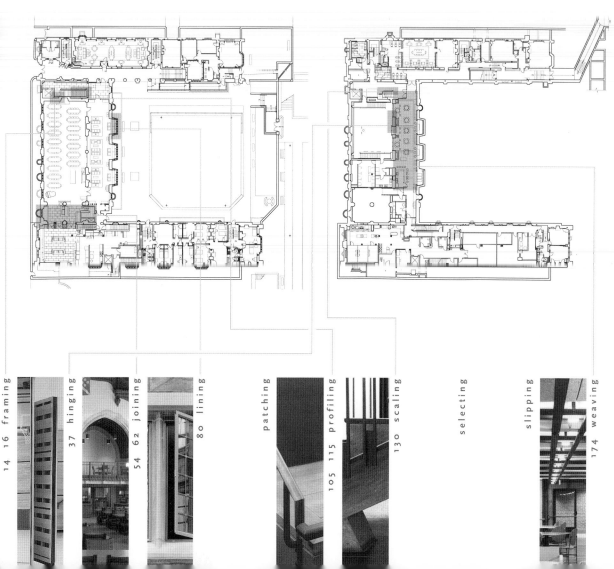

14 16 framing   37 hinging   54 62 joining   80 lining   patching   105 115 profiling   130 scaling   selecting   slipping   174 weaving

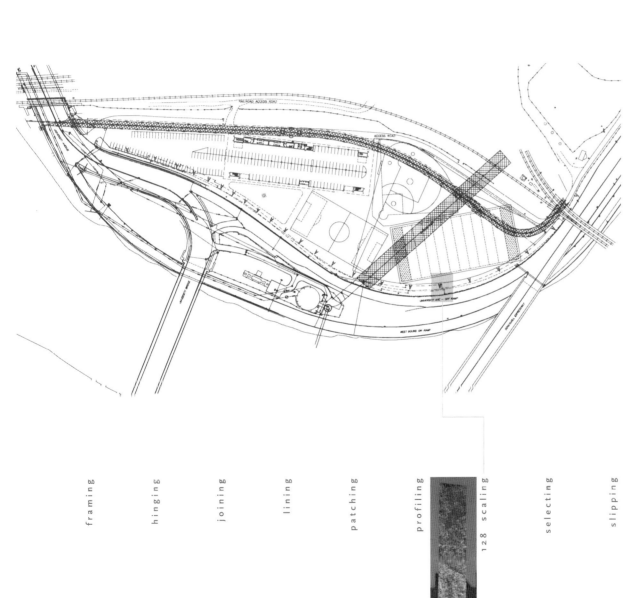

The university sought to define the southeastern campus gateway with a large piece of infrastructure. Our proposal acknowledges the intrinsic contradiction that occurs when an infrastructural background building is called upon to assume a monumental function. No matter how adorned, infrastructure is still infrastructure. We sought to expand the notion of the campus gateway to encompass the entire project site. The strategy acknowledges the encircling highways and railways and the lack of visual connections to the university by arraying a series of pylons along the site's curving perimeter.

framing hinging joining lining patching profiling 128 scaling selecting slipping weaving

Hamilton Village Housing
University of Pennsylvania
1999

The college as a segregated precinct within the city is a well-known American model, and it defines much of urban campus history in this century. The opposite notion of infusing the city throughout the campus, however, is a path less traveled, and offers the vision of a more urbane campus as well as a new college house system unique to the University of Pennsylvania. The ideal of the city in the college house suggests an inversion of the house program space into an open network of social and intellectual opportunity.

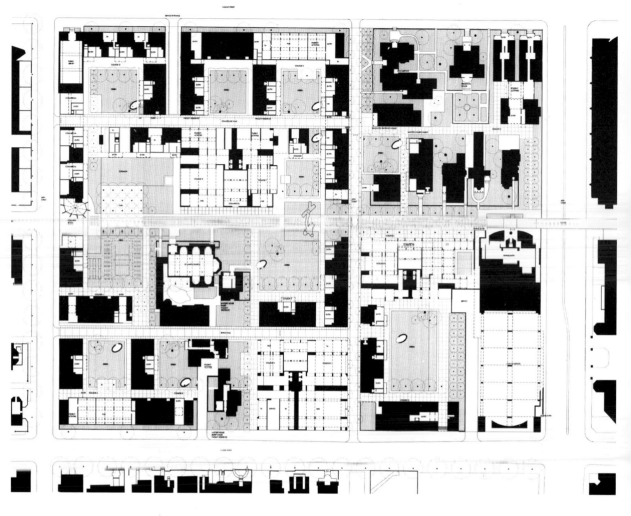

framing   hinging   joining   lining   patching   profiling   scaling   selecting   slipping

162 weaving

206

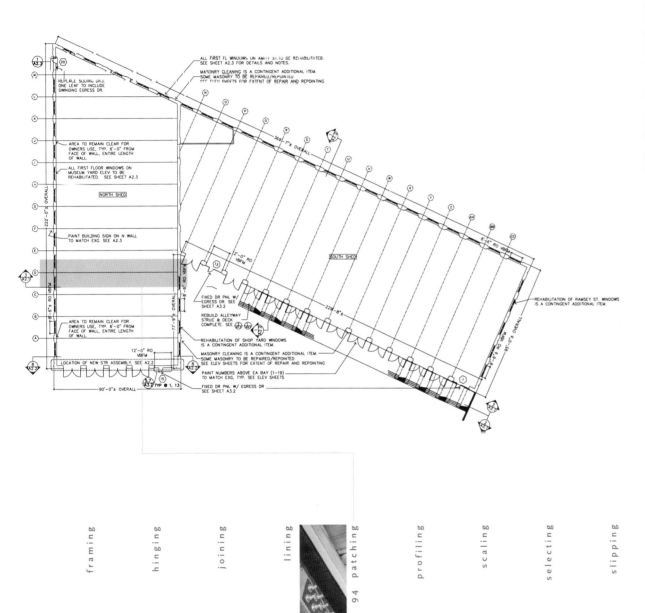

ALL FIRST FL WINDOWS ON AMITY ST. TO BE REHABILITATED.
SEE SHEET A2.3 FOR DETAILS AND NOTES.

MASONRY CLEANING IS A CONTINGENT ADDITIONAL ITEM.
SOME MASONRY TO BE REPAIRED/REPOINTED
SEE ELEV SHEETS FOR EXTENT OF REPAIR AND REPOINTING

REPLACE SLIDING DR.
ONE LEAF TO INCLUDE
SWINGING EGRESS DR.

AREA TO REMAIN CLEAR FOR
OWNERS USE, TYP. 6'-0" FROM
FACE OF WALL, ENTIRE LENGTH
OF WALL.

ALL FIRST FLOOR WINDOWS ON
MUSEUM YARD ELEV TO BE
REHABILITATED. SEE SHEET A2.3

NORTH SHED

PAINT BUILDING SIGN ON N WALL
TO MATCH EXG. SEE A2.3

SOUTH SHED

FIXED DR PNL W/
EGRESS DR SEE
SHEET A3.2

REBUILD ALLEYWAY
STRUC & DECK
COMPLETE. SEE

REHABILITATION OF SHOP YARD WINDOWS
IS A CONTINGENT ADDITIONAL ITEM.

MASONRY CLEANING IS A CONTINGENT ADDITIONAL ITEM.
SOME MASONRY TO BE REPAIRED/REPOINTED
SEE ELEV SHEETS FOR EXTENT OF REPAIR AND REPOINTING

PAINT NUMBERS ABOVE EA BAY (1-19)
TO MATCH EXG. SEE ELEV SHEETS

FIXED DR PNL W/ EGRESS DR
SEE SHEET A3.2

REHABILITATION OF RAMSEY ST. WINDOWS
IS A CONTINGENT ADDITIONAL ITEM.

AREA TO REMAIN CLEAR FOR
OWNERS USE, TYP. 6'-0" FROM
FACE OF WALL, ENTIRE LENGTH
OF WALL.

LOCATION OF NEW STR ASSEMBLY. SEE A2.2

Our analysis showed that by careful modification, we could address the deficiencies that resulted from years of weather while preserving the historical and industrial nature of the building. To lessen the financial bite of rehabilitating the entire building, the museum had us break down the work into phases. Starting with the roof, these projects have been a series of modest interventions to stabilize deterioration.

f r a m i n g

h i n g i n g

j o i n i n g

l i n i n g

9 4   p a t c h i n g

p r o f i l i n g

s c a l i n g

s e l e c t i n g

s l i p p i n g

w e a v i n g

207

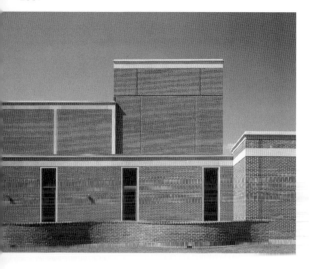

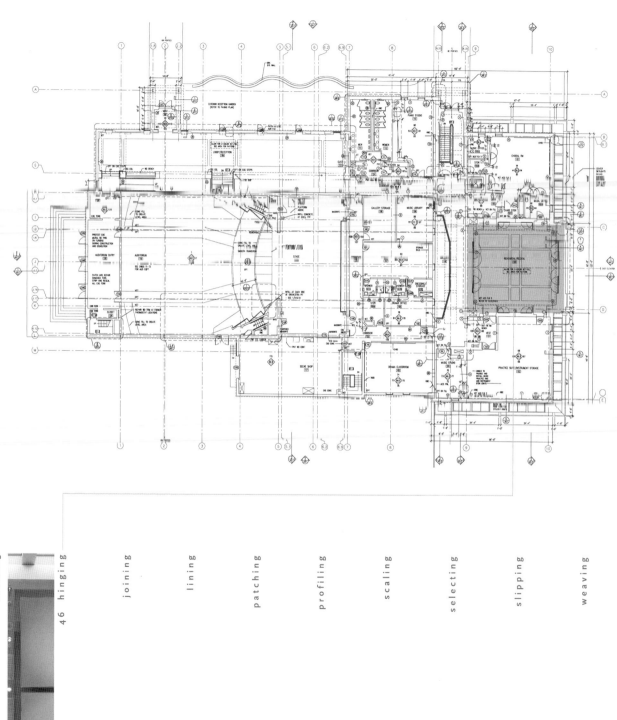

Originally constructed in the 1960s, the Walker Arts Center was in need of an addition and renovation. The completed project transforms the existing building. A new facade and new entrances face the main campus, welcoming students and visitors to an atrium gallery and lobby/reception space. The program contains acoustically designed performance and practice spaces, including a double height recital hall; painting, drawing, printmaking, and sculpture studios; and a fully renovated 500-seat auditorium, with new theatrical systems.

framing 46 hinging joining lining patching profiling scaling selecting slipping weaving

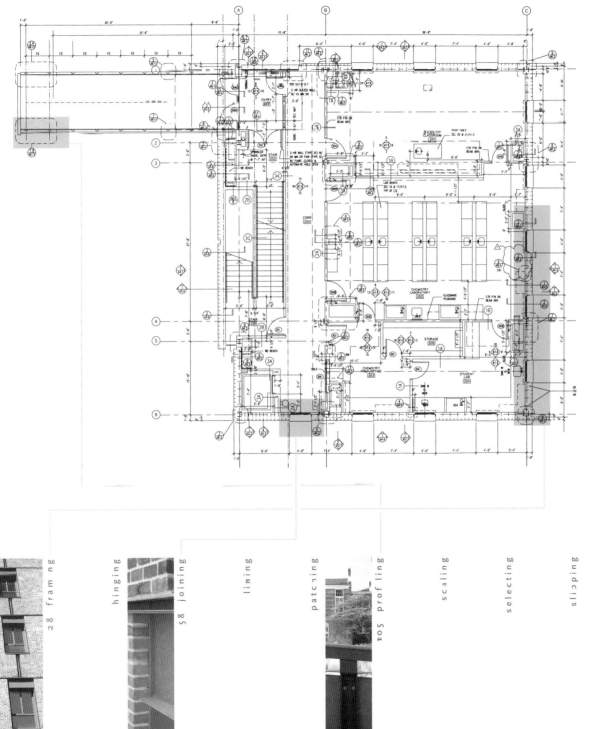

Poly Prep sits in an Olmsted-like park composed of hills, ponds, and a winding road that leads to the school's original 1920s building. The new building partially encloses a courtyard between the original structure and the campus beyond. This upper-class science teaching facility consists of labs with adjacent classrooms and offices. Pressure-equalized brick walls, with aluminum closure trim and windows, form the building envelope. The interior consists of drywall, plaster, and wood, with epoxy resin and slate floors. The bridge leading to the entrance vestibule is steel and slate.

28 framing   hinging   58 joining   lining   patching   105 profiling   scaling   selecting   slipping   weaving

209

A limestone and granite servery addition, projecting into the existing courtyard, is the most outward indication of this renovation of James Gamble Rodgers's historic 1931 complex. In addition, the kitchen was relocated to the basement, and the existing oak-paneled dining hall was outfitted with up-to-date infrastructure. Oak, plaster, and bronze find modern complements in stainless steel, plywood, and slate. Rejecting both an outright mimicry of the existing and the convenient disconnectedness of the new, we sought to join the two ages in a layering of visual depth, formal invention, and material affinity.

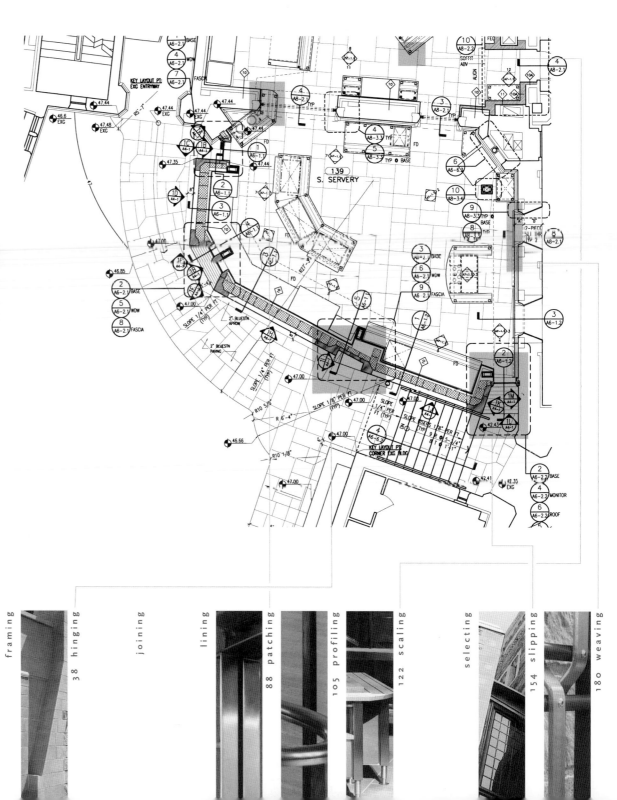

framing   38 hinging   joining   lining   88 patching   105 profiling   122 scaling   selecting   154 slipping   180 weaving

Little Hall was the first dormitory at Princeton to have indoor plumbing. Despite this modern amenity, in the hundred years since construction, its uses and infrastructure have changed. The university had ambitious goals: renovate all the building systems, engage the campus to the west by opening up the ground floor to the adjacent site, provide common facilities, and increase the bed count. The unoccupied basement, previously considered unusable due to its proximity to the railroad (relocated in the 1920s), was seized upon as usable space that would be instrumental to the project.

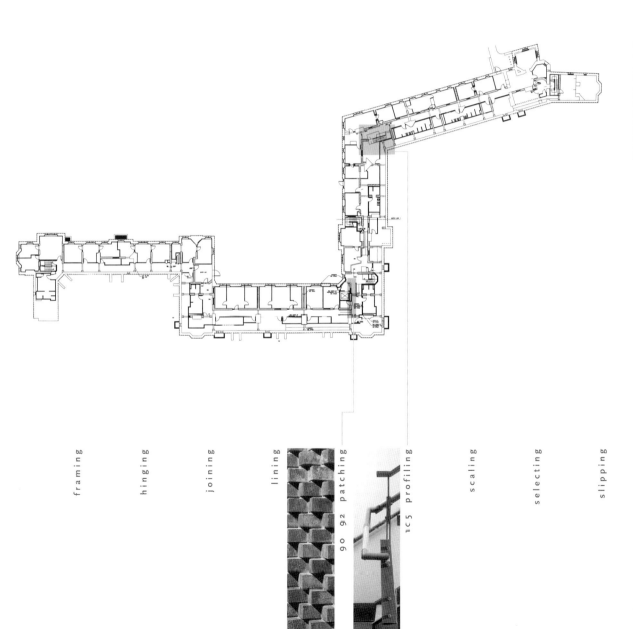

framing   hinging   joining   lining   90 92 patching   105 profiling   scaling   selecting   slipping   weaving

Melvin and Claire Levine Hall
University of Pennsylvania
2002

Transforming this former service yard into an academic quadrangle, Levine Hall provides 50,000 square feet of space for the School of Engineering and Applied Science, housing offices, research labs, and meeting spaces, as well as a 150-seat auditorium. Intended to be a model building for colleges and universities of the twenty-first century, the goal is nonprogrammatically derived spaces and floor plans, which provide long-term flexibility of use and arrangement of space. Accordingly, the floors have been conceived as loftlike, with fourteen-foot floor-to-floor heights, glazed exterior walls, and glazed interior partitions.

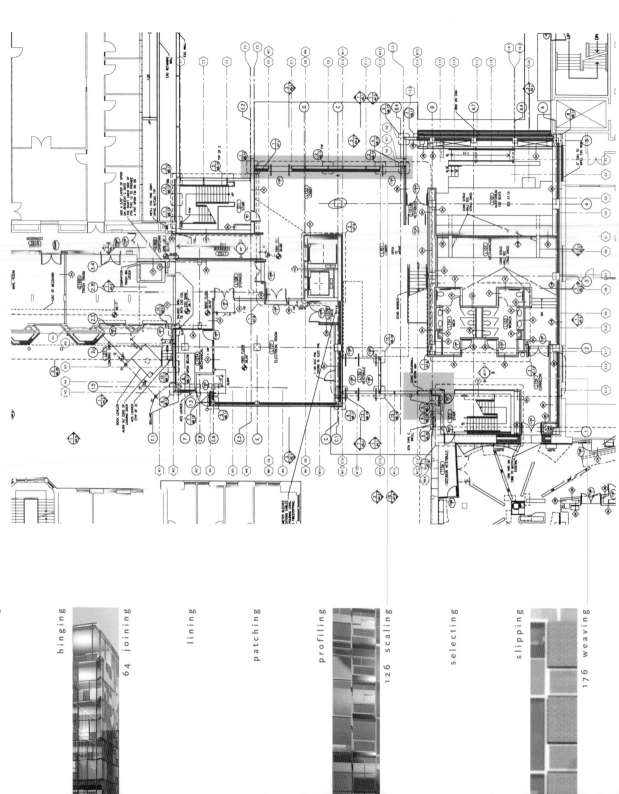

framing   hinging   64 joining   lining   patching   profiling   126 scaling   selecting   slipping   176 weaving

ACKNOWLEDGMENTS

Without a need, and without the means and the willingness to pay for the sheltering of that need, there is no architecture. We think of those who have had the desire and will to work with us to make architecture as our clients. The more ancient but still much used word, patron, embodies a significant hierarchy and inequality in relationship—not based upon collaboration and participation, but instead one of collector and servant—as well as a troubling sense of tolerance on the part of the patron/buyer toward the architect/purveyor. In our clients, we require and receive active, participation and criticism. Our clients in turn demand listening, reaction, and creative options, not preconceptions. Our architecture is a result of this collective creation.

Of special note are those clients who trusted us early based upon little more than instinct. They include Audrey and Joseph Greenberg, Donald and Karlyn Shapiro, Martin Tully, Tom Allingham, Marie and Frank Stufano. Sisters Roberta Rivello and Matthew Anita McDonald, SSJ were among the first to demonstrate the faith with our first campus project. Bill McGarry, along with Harry Bingham entrusted us with two new buildings. Many others, including Fred Moses, Carolyn Raymond, Jeffrey Cornellus, Pamela Delphenich, Terry Nolen, Omar Blaik and Edwardo Glandt, have been extraordinary in their support and commitment to innovative architecture.

Just as patronage is an outmoded term to describe the architect/client relationship, so too are generally held beliefs about attribution. Credit for design is often similarly inconsistent with present practice. Our public relations culture continues to favor heroic singular attribution, perpetuating hopelessly inadequate beliefs about the residence of creativity in one mind despite all the evidence of collective intelligence in other disciplines, and in architecture. Architecture today requires the commitment, knowledge, skill, and passion of many professionals, some of whom are architects, while others belong to specialized disciplines. Our dedicated staff of the last seventeen years, anchored by our associates—Amelia Floresta, Christopher MacNeal, and Richard Malmon—have been the core of our office. They provide leadership, skill, and creative partnership. All of those listed as collaborators have contributed to the growth and development of our work over extended periods of time.

As architects, we draw the lines that represent our intentions. Builders build using those lines for guidance and direction. We owe much of our present and ever developing knowledge of the substance embedded within and beneath the lines to our relationships with countless engineers, construction managers, contractors, fabricators, and suppliers.

Three individuals have made the compilation of Manual possible. George Dodds helped us to start the project. Karl Wallick initiated and extended the organizational framework; he selected, assembled and (re)arranged the images and drawings. He extracted the words from us, both written and spoken. Sarah Williams sharpened them, bringing to the text a master's discipline of the written word as its own craft. Without over a decade of Barry Halkin's photography, we would not have the images to draw from.

Lastly, we owe gratitude to our families for their forbearance, insight and support as we began and continue the struggle to build and grow. Thank you Barbara, Christopher, Caitlin, Marguerite and Harrison for staying with us when we should have been with you.

213

COLLABORATORS

Stephen Kieran

James Timberlake

Samuel Harris

Barbara Kreuter

George Dodds

Beth Eichler

Richard Gladstone

Greg Hall

Mark Brahaney

Ellen Doney

Ann Leopold

Christoff Raciborski

Adam Yarinsky

Dianna Noya

David Achtenberg

Margo Angevine

Paula Stonesifer

Scott Wing

J.V. DeSousa

Patreese Martin

James Wallace

Deborah Wartluft

Truett Roberts

John Dasilva

Margaret Kieran

Rose Spadea

David Thurman

Christopher Macneal

Beth Baranoski

Richard Maimon

Fran Hegeler

David McCullough

Ila Burdette

Robin Eaton

Amy Floresta

Richard Hodge

Mary Tucker

Charles Waldheim

Tamarah Long

Claire Donato

Whitney Morrill

Melanie Swick

Michael Williamson

Steven Irvine

Margaret Gardiner

Charles Horak

Lisa Mattern

Martha Finney

Leslie WellmanMcRae

John Poros

Jennifer Kinkead

David Hess

Quing-Yun Ma

Richard Blender

Mark Johnson

Chris Panfil

Polly Rocray

James Poteet

Sean O'Brien

Brian Cannon

Kishwar Rizvi

Pam Zimmerman

Amy Stein

Tony Weber

Anne Hicks

Jane Pfaff

Maribel Beas

Lisa Waterman

Geogy Dolgy

Julia Czerniak

Chariss McAfee

Lené Copeland

Gina Rodzon

Nancy Wu Downing

Gwendolyn Michell

Todd Ray

L.B. Young

Dana Reed

Alice Tufel

Melissa Vaughan

James Unkefer

Honey Zoerkler

Elizabeth Thornton

Amanda Sachs

Kimberley Jones

Jason E. Smith

Catherine Hillman

Mark Jackson

Pat Ward

Patty Bechard

Anne Roderer

Judith Kennedy

Cathy Moy

Ron Crawford

Yves Gauthier

Marie Reichardt

Eric Rzeszut

Steven Johns

Lisa Neely

Crystal Trotman

Peter Vieira

Kevin Rasmussen

Albert Garcia

Ian Kell

Jeanne Sliwinski

Vanessa Keith

Elizabeth McDonald

Joel Young

Todd Margasak

Krisada Surichamari

Kurtran Wright

Nicole Stafford

Linh Tran

Alejandro Salazar

Nicole Rittenour

Christiane Arnouts

Karen Moustafellos

Marceli Botticelli

Samuel Robinson

Kay Souksamlane

Jean Won

Marc Kushner

Clifton Fordham

David Mark Riz

Alix Peck

Todd Hoehn

Craig Morton

Allison Garwood

Christopher M. Pfiffner

William Craig

Monica Wyatt

Kannikar Petersen

Sarah Devlin

Hazami Sayed

Jill Desimini

Matthew Neiman

Andre Smith

Nicholas Fiore

John Mueller

Marisa Clark

Andrea Quilici

Matthew Sauer

Karl Wallick

Rageshwar Wilcox

Colleen McGlone

Richard Snyder

Brian Carney

Todd Berreth

Frank Dominiano

Nicole LaRossa

Sarika Bajoria

Janice Wang

Mark Sanderson

Vera Parlac

Meiko Sato

Jules Dingle

Eugene Chung

Allison Hsiao

John Franklin

Kohei Sasakawa

Gabriel Biller

Rocelyn Dee

Heewon Park

Brian Murphy

Castor Kong

Eric Delss

Justin Doull

Jeff Goldstein

Elisheva Levi

Mary Ellen Bealor

Jeanne Aquilino

Jonathan Fallet

Lorraine Kodumal

Eulalia Hartung

Mary Lou Bergh

Adrienne Swiatocha

PHOTOGRAPHERS

Robert Benson: 55

Tom Bernard: 45, 60, 76, 77, 78, 97, 114, 139, 157, 165, 166, 167

Barry Halkin: front cover, 14, 15, 16, 17, 18, 19, 20, 21, 26, 27, 29, 36, 37, 38, 39, 40, 41, 42, 43, 46, 47, 49, 52, 53, 54, 56, 58, 59, 62, 63, 68, 69, 70, 72, 73, 74, 75, 80, 84, 88, 89, 90, 91, 92, 94, 95, 99, 102, 103, 104, 105, 106, 107, 112, 113, 114, 115, 118, 119, 121, 122, 123, 125, 126, 128, 129, 131, 140, 142, 143, 144, 145, 148, 149, 152, 153, 155, 159, 162, 170, 171, 173, 174, 175, 178, 179, 180, 181, back cover

Jack Ramsdale & Barry Halkin: 2, 36, 82, 83

Catherine Tighe: 25, 30, 31, 36, 57, 78, 79, 103, 108, 109, 114, 115, 132, 133, 136, 137, 141, 150, 151, 156, 166, 168, 169,

KTA: 22, 23, 24, 28, 32, 33, 44, 61, 88, 96, 98, 120, 124, 130, 152, 154, 164, 172

Published by

Princeton Architectural Press

37 East Seventh Street

New York, New York 10003

For a free catalog of books, call 1.800.722.6657.

Visit our web site at www.papress.com.

Printed and bound in China

05 04 03 02   5 4 3 2 1 First edition

Editor: Jennifer N. Thompson

Designer: Karl Wallick

Proofreader: Lauren Neefe

Special thanks to: Nettie Aljian, Ann Alter, Amanda Atkins,
Nicola Bednarek, Janet Behning, Megan Carey, Penny Chu,
Jan Cigliano, Jane Sheinman, Clare Jacobson, Mark Lamster,
Nancy Eklund Later, Linda Lee, Evan Schoninger, Lottchen
Shivers, and Deb Wood of Princeton Architectural Press
—Kevin C. Lippert, publisher

Library of Congress Cataloging-in-Publication Data

Kieran, Stephen, 1951-, Timberlake, James, 1952-
 Manual, the architecture of KieranTimberlake / introduction
by Alberto Pérez-Gómez ; Stephen Kieran & James
Timberlake.-- 1st ed.
   p. cm.
 ISBN 1-56898-313-1 (pbk. : alk paper)
 1. KieranTimberlake (Firm) 2. Architecture--United States--
20th
century--Designs and plans. 3. Architecture--Details. I. Title:
Manual. II. Title: Architecture of KieranTimberlake. III. Title:
Architecture of Kieran Timberlake. IV. Timberlake, James,
1952- V.
Title.
 NA737.K49 K53 2002
 721--dc21

                    2001005989